ANCIENT FRIENDSHIP FOR MODERN MEN

How to Build Lasting Friendships & Adventures from Ancient Ideas

Don Owens

ISBN 979-8-9859232-4-7 *(paperback)*
    979-8-9859232-5-4 *(epub)*

Unless otherwise indicated, Scripture quotations are taken from the Holy Bible, New International Version®, NIV® Copyright ©1973, 1978, 1984, 2011 by Biblica, Inc.® Used by permission. All rights reserved worldwide.

Scripture quotations marked NKJV are taken from the New King James Version®. Copyright © 1982 by Thomas Nelson. Used by permission. All rights reserved.

Editing, formatting, and design are by ChristianEditingAndDesign.com Illustration and cover by Don Owens.

For my best friend, Danae Owens,
and the men of The May Club

.

CONTENTS

"To whom am I to present my pretty little book, freshly smoothed off with dry pumice-stone! To you Cornelius: for you used to think that my trifles were worth something, long ago, when you took courage, you alone of Italians, to set forth the whole history of the world in three volumes, learned volumes, by Jupiter, and laborious wrought. So take and keep for your own this little book, such as it is, and whatever it is worth; and may it, O Virgin my patroness, live and last for more than one century."

— Gaius Valerius Catullus[1]

---

1   Catullus, *The Poems of Gaius Valerius Catullus* (Cambridge, MA: Harvard University Press, 1962; reprinted with corrections, 2017), 3.

PREFACE

Social media, metaverses, and mobile devices have made the world a lonelier place—the exact opposite of our expectations from technology. You'd think these gizmos would bring men together, but it seems men are struggling these days, especially when it comes to building meaningful relationships. The modern age has further degraded the opportunity to connect. Online gaming, ubiquitous pornography, hookup culture, social media posts, and hundreds of sports channels and apps are not improving our lives.

Men need support and advice related to building their relationships, succeeding in marriage, raising children, managing their work environments and careers, and finding purpose and meaning in friends, family, and work. They need adventure in their lives and individuals to share in the stories. Men need mentors to guide them and pupils in whom they may invest their knowledge and time. But who will guide them into meaningful relationships?

One of the most important journeys in my life has been the journey of friendship with other men. It was a journey of discovering brotherhood, losing friends, and rediscovering brotherhood again through living with intentionality.

As I walked the path of developing friendships, I also discovered ancient friends in the old books left for us to discover. I discovered countless books, sermons, seminars, and websites addressing how to build friendship, but I learned along the way the ancients had much to say about friendship, and they said it better and more directly.

I connected on an intimate level with the pain of Boethius, the wisdom of Cicero, and the reflections of Plato even though they lived thousands of years before me. Their words provided paths for meeting and serving others in my lifetime.

The noise of the modern age is so loud and the visual and audio inputs so numerous it is hard to hear the teachings of the ancients. If we read and reflect on the lives and wisdom of those in the past, we will find them much like us and with answers to our burning questions.

My first hope in this short read is that you might choose to join me in the pursuit of others and build your own intentional approach to offering friendship to those you encounter. My other goal is for you to discover the gifts of ancient political leaders, philosophers, religious leaders, and poets and want to pursue their works, which have so much meaning for modern living.

In service,

Don Owens

April 18, 2023

Chapter 1

A WINTER'S GHOST

IT APPEARED MY WORLD WAS TURNED UPSIDE DOWN.
Everyone I knew would continue without me. Everything
before me was unknown and exaggerated to the greatest
negative results in my mind. All the events that had made it
possible for me to feel a part of a community were for naught.

I was fifteen years old. In July 1985, my father was transferred
by his company from Oak Brook, Illinois, to Fort Worth, Texas.
Apparently, he and the president of the company were not able
to get along. Strangely enough, my father traveled frequently
with his work, yet not even distance from his boss made for a
functional relationship. Dad was good at what he did—he was
an excellent salesman and manager—so keeping him around
but creating separation must have been the plan.

I remember when my parents sat my brother and me down
to share the news. It was in the last days of my freshman year
of high school, and I had just returned home on the school
bus. My parents asked my brother and me to join them in the

11

dining room, the place of all formal announcements, good and bad. I was concerned about the reason, as the last time we had a sit-down in the formal dining room, it was to discuss my algebra grades.

My father's tone was somber but hopeful. "We are making a change with my job and are looking at moving to Fort Worth, Texas. It's a great city, and we'll be buying a bigger home. I think you'll like Texas."

I was immediately shaken, but I spoke up anyway. "All they have are tumbleweeds and horses in Texas, and all my friends are here."

My parents offered sympathy and agreed changes would not be easy, but they assured us everything would work out. I was not convinced.

And with that, we took our first trip to Texas in May of 1985 to look for a home. Fort Worth was old and drab, with very little downtown activity. This was a shock after seven years growing up around the hustle and bustle of Chicago. I remember our first couple of nights in Fort Worth. We stayed across from the Water Gardens. There was barely a soul walking the streets, and I guess I missed the sights and sounds of the city. I feared this would be a huge disaster.

After checking out a few houses, my parents purchased a spec home, which was to be completed by August. We celebrated, and my father gave my brother and me some champagne. This made us feel like grownups, sure, but I think he was trying to distract us from our growing anxieties. My parents had also announced we would be going on vacation to Hawaii for two weeks in July. At any rate, the champagne seemed benign enough, and we laughed and had a good time. However, in the end, I drank enough to make me sick the next day.

Looking back now at that fifteen-year-old kid, I remember his mind was racing with the fears of all things new. Yes, I was a dweeby kid. I had just had my braces taken off, had acne, and wore dark thick glasses. I didn't know how to pick out any stylish clothes, and my hair made me look like a rejected Beatle. I took what teasing I got, but somehow I was able to build two great groups of friends. The hollowness I felt when leaving Chicago undoubtedly had to do with leaving them. Indeed, I missed those at my high school, Glenbard South, and those on the other side of Wheaton, Illinois, at the church we attended. My school friends were mostly Catholic and attended church elsewhere. I was the lone Baptist in our group.

My faith was centric to my life at a young age. I was bold for a kid and brought my Bible to school, keeping it on my desk on full display. I led a Bible study during lunch hour once a week, where I was pleased to talk about Jesus with my simple theological understandings. In the 1980s this got some attention, but not much.

At the same time, because this group of friends at Glenbard South didn't know my friends from church, I tended to sample some of the worldly things I found curious. You know, the things teenage boys are always interested in: girls, cigarettes, and Playboy magazines. This may sound tame to a young person today who has access to the world on their cellphone, but remember, times were different in the '80s. However, I still felt as if I were living a double life as a believer and a curious teenage boy. At times in my young life, I felt much guilt over my behavior. For example, when I was fourteen, one of my schoolmates came over when my parents were out, and we made a solid dent in my father's vodka, later stumbling about the neighborhood all evening. If I had been Catholic, I would have been in confession the next morning, and maybe this would have been good for my consistent feelings of guilt.

I carried this guilt with me to the other side of town where my core group of friends lived. We had all grown up around each other from about nine years of age, and these young men were the people I looked up to. I wanted to be like them. Although they were young, it appeared they had it all together. They were on fire for their faith and seemed to live out their lives as Christians as if it were part of their DNA. They were kind, inclusive, and knew how to have good clean fun. We went to concerts and the parks, hung out, and ate lunches and dinners at each other's homes. They were available and encouraging. They were everything I felt I was not, yet here I was hanging out with them regularly.

There was this amazing turning point in our friendships during my eighth-grade year—a moment that solidified our connections. Our church had a winter retreat at a camp in Michigan in an area along the shores of Lake Michigan with massive sand dunes. The winter snows were abundant, and we hiked, sledded, and tubed. The stage was set to have a wonderful time with my regular friends, but I also got to meet older kids. This was one of the first times I had been around high school kids. They seemed so much older and more mature. In my mind, some of the seniors seemed to be the size of Goliath, but they were approachable, supportive, and kind.

I enjoyed getting to know the older kids, but this isn't what made this trip different. You see, I had a visit from the Holy Spirit. Now, if you're not a Christian, stay with me. You can ascribe your names to some of these experiences or a psychoanalysis if you wish.

As a Christian, I believe in the Holy Spirit, but as a young person, I did not have a strong intellectual understanding or a wealth of experiences. For those who don't know, the Holy Spirit in Christianity is a being who makes up a triune God—the Father, the Son, and the Holy Spirit. They act and think together but perform different roles in their relationship with each other and those outside of themselves. But let me get back to the story. . . .

I was sitting in a session at camp when I felt something come over me. We had gathered in the main lodge of the camp, which smelled of burnt firewood from decades past. The folding chairs were cold and in no particular order. The youth minister standing up front was challenging us to have an encounter with God, to seek his face as we prayed. He asked us to consider how we lived out the love of Jesus in our families and friendships.

The room was quiet except for some individuals praying aloud, and then I began to do the same. A few of my friends gathered around, and we prayed together. In that very moment, I felt God's Spirit in a unique way. My friends shared the experience with me, as if we were being pushed to the ground. We continued to pray but now were on our knees with our hands on each other's shoulders.

The entire room had moved into small groups like ours—four or five young people gathered and praying, hugging, crying, and laughing. People in the various groups began to stand up and hug one another—so did we. I felt led to go over and start playing the piano on the far side of the meeting room, so I played and sang a song I knew by Ronnie Milsap: "What a Difference You've Made in My Life." And one by one, my peers came over to the piano and started singing along. I was soon surrounded by people locking arms and swaying as they sang.

I was in disbelief—amazed that anything I was doing would bring a room of people together in a shared experience. But there I was with my friends, these grown-up high school kids, and having an existential experience. It was as if God were showing his greatness, and I was compelled to be low, as if before a throne. I don't imagine anyone else remembers that night like I do—if they remember it at all.

Flash forward thirty-five years. It turned out our youth pastor, Steve French, had someone videotaping this session on one of those gargantuan VCR cameras. He posted the video of the moment to Facebook just a few years ago, and I saw it for the first time in 2020. Every emotion rushed back to me. I was amazed there was a visual recording of a moment so important to me. This was the defining moment of my entire life. I didn't know it at the time, but it would set the stage for my most important pursuits.

The things that had occurred afterward were not on the VCR tape. We had talked all night, and I had felt I had discovered something new in my faith, along with forming unique and deeper friendships. My close circle of eighth- grade friends bonded in a special way, and we all agreed we were done with handshakes and superficial types of gestures; hence, we decided we would greet each other with a hug from now on whenever we met at church. We determined that true friends should greet each other with a holy hug because we most certainly weren't going to greet each other with a holy kiss.

Over the next year, our friendships grew. We would talk through all the trials and troubles that seem so big to young people; we truly supported one another. I don't know if our style of friendship was unique at fourteen years of age, but it sure seemed like it to me. I was always so energized after long conversations outside the roller rink, or a Bible study at McDonald's, or a Wednesday night at church. I felt truly blessed.

Over the next year I was amazed and grateful that I had such a supportive circle of friends—grateful to be part of a youth group with strong leadership and to have friends at school. But oh, how things change . . . my parents wrecked my world when they made that fateful announcement that we would be moving.

Of course, I hold no animosity toward my parents today, but then I was bitter toward them. We returned from the two-week trip to Hawaii in the middle of July. My father went to Texas to begin work and ensure our home was set for completion. My mother took my brother and me to Georgia, where all our extended family lived, and we finished out the rest of summer break there before heading to Texas on August 15.

My friends had planned a going away party at Tim Tanner's home a couple of days before we left Wheaton. If I remember correctly, the group included Tim Tanner, Tim Simcox, Doug Rummel, Keith Johnson, and me. We had all planned to stay the night. It was to be an evening of food, hanging out, and talking about girls. Doug was dating a girl named Ruth at the time, and we were probably all a bit jealous because she was super cute.

At some point in the evening as I sat listening, it struck me— this was my last night with the guys. It was like getting hit with an emotional baseball bat to the back of the head. Remember, this was the '80s, long before Facebook and Instagram and WhatsApp. We had mail, which took two weeks to deliver, and long-distance phone calls, which were limited because of the cost.

At any rate, I remember I went outside on the front porch and just cried my eyes out. I knew those friendships were over—

nothing like this would happen again. I couldn't believe my parents would do this to me. I cried out, "Why?" to God and sat there feeling so extremely alone.

I don't know how long I was out there on the porch. Tim Simcox must have noticed I was gone and came looking for me. He sat down next to me, and I voiced all the thoughts in my head through my tears. I wasn't embarrassed. We'd sat together at Sunday school, Taco Bell and McDonald's, each other's homes, and countless church events. We were real friends, and I needed to get it all out. I felt as though these connections were all about to be lost.

Tim was an incredible example to me of living out your faith, and his actions were much more mature than mine—more thoughtful. Here's a good example of his character: The summer before, we had decided to meet in downtown Wheaton and go see a movie. When we got there, we found out the movie was rated PG-13. Tim's parents didn't let him go to PG-13 movies, so he told me he couldn't go in. I went anyway—what a lousy friend I was.

Here's another example: We went on a college tour trip the next June. On the trip were some girls I had never met. I was currently dating someone at Glenbard South, but on the trip, I started making out with another girl. Tim sat me down and said my actions were not cool, and I needed to get my love life in order.

He was a good friend when I was not.

So back to the porch. We sat there. Tim didn't give me any answers or suggestions—he just listened and put his arm around my neck and hugged me. We must have sat there in silence for twenty minutes.

Tim was a hero that night. What fifteen-year-old knows how to comfort someone by just listening and being present? His example over the years and that evening before I was to leave Wheaton forever burned into my mind an image of true friendship.

Tim's kindness, the night at winter camp, and my faith in Jesus and encounter with the Holy Spirit were the catalysts of one of my life's major pursuits . . . which is to intentionally build friendships.

I will never forget Tim. Following his example, I have spent my life looking for opportunities to comfort others, especially when their world is turned completely upside down. Yet now I am grateful my world was turned upside down because it is from this purview I began pursuing deep friendships with others. Sometimes all it takes is a little perspective to turn the tide of your life.

Chapter 2

REDISCOVERY

W HEN MY FAMILY MOVED TO FORT WORTH, I WAS CERTAIN I WOULD NEVER KNOW FRIENDS LIKE THOSE I HAD LEFT IN CHICAGO. I battled a host of questions: *How do I go about recreating relationships like the ones I had back home? How can I keep from resenting others or becoming bitter when other friendships don't add up or, worse, fail? Is it even possible to add and manage additional friendships? How many friends can one person navigate anyway?*

There is so much a fifteen-year-old can't know about the world. My life was full of fear that my best moments were behind me. At any rate, the search for true friendship would set the stage for something great in my life—and I hope the lives of others.

We arrived in Texas on August 15, 1985. It was 105 degrees when I opened the door at the Holiday Inn South on I-35. I was angry from the get-go. We drove over to our home, and I found everything I could wrong with the house. In fact, I found fault with everything. I was not easy to live with—I realize that now.

I made life hard for my parents for the better part of a year and a half. I was outright rebellious. I sneaked out of the house many nights. I hid and used alcohol. I would purposely avoid communication with my parents. When I did talk to them, it was to complain about them, about school, or just generally about Texas.

When I started my sophomore year a few weeks later, I found out at school and church I had a chance to start fresh. I had no history in my new surroundings, so I was not relegated to a group. I wasn't the dweeby kid of my late middle school and freshman years. Soon I'd lost the dark glasses and changed to contacts. More up-to-date clothes and hairstyle followed.

Over the next year, I built a network of acquaintances—no close friends, but people who were very different from my previous crowd. A few of the jocks even liked to hang out with me for some reason—also a few stoners who somehow thought I was chill. Dressing a little preppy seemed to get me some access to party invitations and various social circles, including church.

First Baptist Church in Crowley, Texas, became our new church. The youth group and youth pastor were kind people. Unlike in Chicago, almost everyone at church went to the same school, so I had frequent church interaction with my classmates.

It seemed relationships existed simply for social interactions. Probably like many at that age, I was more concerned with dating in those years. By the time my senior year came around, I had met Danae LeMond, whom I would marry six years later. Marriage was on our radar early on, even though we still had much yet to figure out about life.

Danae and I married in June 1993. One new thing this brought into our lives was "couple friends." Typically, the next couple of years, friends came with their spouses. This was the case even in 1995 when I still thought frequently about my early friendships. I missed them and I wanted to recreate those types of close friendships if possible. I had lost touch with my friends in Chicago over the years. The old crew was now divided across the country, but it seemed the example Tim had set never left me. I wanted to be a good friend and perhaps make these couple friendships less superficial.

David and Rachel Rutherford were one pair of our couple friends. We spent much time with them, as we went to the same church and lived in the same apartment complex. At the end of May, I invited him to go with me on a long weekend of camping and hiking in Lincoln National Forest in New Mexico. He accepted. This trip would be the catalyst I was looking for to begin building unique and treasured friendships over the next three decades.

I was working in radio in Dallas in May of 1995 and didn't get off until late, so David said he would pick me up, and we would make the trip to New Mexico through the night. We drove through the dark with the radio blasting, turning it up and down with the conversation. Often, we rolled down the windows. I felt free from work and was glad to have a weekend break. David was even more excited to get away because he had a young daughter at home. Together, we were escaping our lives for a moment.

"It is really hard being a dad," David shared. "It is nonstop. With both Rachel and me working, there is nothing left at the end of the day for the baby or for each other."

"I don't know about being a father yet, but it is hard enough to keep a marriage moving in the right direction," I responded. "It seems as if we work all the time. When we are home, we are just angry the other person is there. With working so much, I even forgot about my first wedding anniversary. I was reminded when I got home from the office at midnight. As I slid into bed, my hand hit a card under the pillow. The second my hand hit it, I knew I had screwed up."

David offered some affirmation. "Yeah, but this is just a busy season of life, I guess. Building a family and career —a little forgetfulness must be okay."

Our conversation continued to weave in and out of the music as we attempted to solve our problems and those of the world. Open about what we were feeling, we were truly seeking to support or provide advice in each discussion.

"I've been working at this job for only a few months in north Dallas, and I don't think it's going to work out," I shared. "It's an interesting gig, but I don't see the vision."

"You need to get back into local radio again," David suggested. "You get to do more variety instead of just marketing."

"Maybe I should." Spurred on by this conversation, just one week later I began sending out resumes and looking for a job back in local radio—and I found one.

In the early morning hours, the conversation did wane as we closed in on our destination. Arriving south of Cloudcroft, New Mexico, around five in the morning, we drove his Honda Civic down gravel roads looking for a place to pitch a tent and get a little sleep. We were nervous because we had lost a tire a few hours earlier and were running on a spare. We weren't sure how well the spare was going to hold on the rough roads.

Picking a spot near some massive pine trees, we set up the tent and quickly fell asleep. After a short sleep, we woke up just as the sun was coming up over one of the ridges. It was beautiful. Speechless, we watched the sunrise. After grabbing our hiking gear, water, and snacks, we headed out for the day. We walked and talked, occasionally sitting down to rest.

Sitting quietly was new to me then. I hadn't yet realized how important those times are—or how much I would enjoy them. Now I know the great joy in sitting quietly with someone you trust and sharing a moment without words.

On that trip, David and I both appreciated the quiet as we listened to the wind blowing through the trees and watched the sun setting over the mountain. It was a worship experience watching God's craftsmanship in action. By his grace, we were permitted to enjoy it in much the same way he does. I can see God sitting quietly, taking pleasure in just looking at what he made.

Upon returning to camp, we built a fire and cooked ribs. As we discussed family life, politics, and religion, we realized our ideas aligned. It seemed to me I had found a close friend again. We agreed we would take another trip the next May. We also decided to invite more guys to join us.

I realized by the second year that our trip in May was a way to build experiences and develop friendships. We named it "The May Club." Every May we head out for five days of hiking, climbing, fishing, kayaking, and countless more excursions. We generally stay in a large lodge and enjoy evenings of food, drinks, games, and laughs. We have done this successfully now for twenty-eight years—we are a camp recreated for adults.

The conversations that have taken place through all the fun have been amazing—sharing life experiences, problems, and solutions; debating politics and faith; creating new connections and new opportunities; and simply enjoying the company of others.

The May Club has really been successful. Most years the trip has included twenty-five to forty men. A total of one hundred guys have attended over our twenty-eight years.

To make things interesting, we added a die-hard trip most years for the extra adventurous in the group. This may include climbing a mountain or hiking in remote places. Even during this more adventurous time, most of the men, as David and I had done on that first trip, have good conversations in the wilderness.

On the first May Club trip with David, I was twenty-five years old, a newbie husband who would be a father within a year and a half. It was great to have a friend to confide in as I was building a career and learning to be a dad. But as life goes, my friendship with David would have a season of closeness that would change as we pursued different interests.

David came to The May Club most years until about 2009, when the demands of his job as a church pastor would pull him from old circles. We occasionally checked in on each other. We always found it easy to pick up where we had left off.

In 2021, David became ill and was unable to recover. He died in September of that year. His passing was an undefinable loss for his family and his church family. He was a kind man. I never heard him raise his voice even when he was angry. He encouraged all those around him and was a comforter. He was selfless and giving. I truly miss him and am most saddened when I reflect on his never being able to join us on a May Club trip again.

I've shared about Tim and David and their powerful impacts on my life because they were shining examples of friendships that influenced me so much. As I became more intentional in the pursuit of other relationships, I also received assistance from friends I never met in person but learned from their writings—individuals who, long before me, considered the dynamics of friendship in a way I never could have done without their help. Men like Aristotle, Marcus Tullius Cicero, and Thomas Aquinas—the ancients.

From the examples of Tim and David, from the well-developed thoughts of the ancients, and from my own experiences, I began the journey of intentionally pursuing others from a desire to recreate the incredible connections I had experienced as a kid and out of loneliness as an adult. I learned the pursuit of others is less about solving your emptiness and more about helping others with the emptiness they feel.

In today's world, people desperately need true friendship. The technology designed to bring us all closer together is instead driving us further apart. Social media is used as a soapbox that never enlightens. It generally creates anger and factions, which lead to separation from anyone who thinks differently. Take, for example, the Facebook posts that portray us all living the perfect life even when we are fully aware of our own trials. Typically, our resentment grows toward those who appear to have it all together.

Other technologies create more distractions and cause us to spend less time in the presence of others. More and more people now take classes online, work from home, and have countless items delivered to their front door to avoid going out. It's easy to become cloistered.

And don't forget about online gaming! It is now a social event as participants build their world or fight their enemies, but seldom will anyone build a deep relationship with their distant comrade or opponent in a virtual environment.

People are waiting longer to get married. In doing so, they delay some of the elements that mature us in our relationships with others. Career growth or self-fulfillment become the goals before making commitments or caring for others. This selfish approach then infects our perspective of others throughout life as we put personal wants before the needs of others or view marriage and children as burdensome.

We are a much more mobile society than in the past, making it easy to pick up and move far away from the familiar. Moves can be made with great frequency. The pandemic has made it possible for us to "work from anywhere." A culture of van-life has people in constant motion, offering amazing scenery through the open back doors of a van along with a picture of a perfectly made vegan taco. Relationships are viewed as brief encounters instead of developing and deepening friendships.

Parents are spending more time than ever before with only their children. Select sports and endless school functions and limited vacation time have parents forgoing friendships to shuffle children about. And to avoid guilt, they attend every function. Sons don't get to see their fathers laugh, talk, and drink with their adult friends to provide the children with healthy examples of companionship and fun.

Boy Scouts, Indian Guides, Awana groups, and other clubs that used to bring the generations together are fading away due to cultural shifts and, in part, due to a failure to deal with the horrible events of child abuse by outliers.

Our social clubs are vanishing.

According to the Survey Center of American Life,[2] the number of people who say they have no close friends grew to 12 percent in 2021 from 3 percent in 1990. In 1990, 33 percent of people surveyed said they had ten or more close friends, and in 2021, only 13 percent. In 1990, 75 percent said they had a best friend. In 2021, only 59 percent reported having a best friend.

Our politics also drive us further apart. Of the Republicans surveyed, 53 percent reported having Democrat friends, while only 32 percent of the Democrats surveyed reported having Republican friends.[3]

---

2   Daniel A. Cox, "The State of American Friendship: Change, Challenges, and Loss," Survey Center on American Life, published June 8, 2021, https://www.americansurveycenter.org/research/the-state-of-american-friendship-change-challenges-and-loss/.

3   Cox, "State of American Friendship."

The divisiveness of this world has made friendship a rare bird, yet friendship is a key ingredient to living a full life. Humans are all clearly made to be in relationships. We are dependent on one another to simply survive in the world. Humans need other humans to learn. Humans need other humans to feel fulfilled. Humans need other humans to share in experiences.

We need each other.

A few blessed souls have a large personality, great intelligence, or extreme talent that causes the world to flock to be with them, but this is not true for most of us. And even if people flock to you, life can remain a lonely journey of shallow connections.

If you ever have a sense of loneliness or feel a lack of deep friendships, you are far from alone. Few people know what to do about these feelings or how to pursue deeper relationships. However, if we sit and wait for relationships to find us, we may miss out on incredible experiences and opportunities to serve others. The intentional pursuit of others is such a noble pursuit, the ancients dwelt upon it and provided patterns for success. The process is not clinical or formulaic but must always include finding a purpose and a sincerity to serve others, sometimes by replicating examples from the past. We can review, for example, the relationships of King David and Jonathan, John Adams and Thomas Jefferson, Mark Twain and Nikola Tesla, as well as J. R. R. Tolkien and C. S. Lewis. They all had one thing in common: These men made friendship with one another a priority. Therefore, we can safely rely on this corollary: Friendship begins with the intentional pursuit of others.

Chapter 3

DAMON AND PYTHIAS

DIONYSIUS WAS A RUTHLESS, UNKIND TYRANT WHO RULED SYRACUSE ON THE ISLAND OF SICILY. He had gained the throne through scheming and bribery. Once he ascended as ruler, he was cruel to the people of Syracuse and to strangers. He was irrational and unpredictable, and no one wanted to cross his path.

One evening the ruler had a dream in which a local townsman named Pythias attempted to take his life and his throne. When Dionysius awoke, he had Pythias arrested and sentenced to death for treason, believing if he dreamed it, it must be true.

Pythias had no way to prove his innocence against the king's false claims, but he did make a request of Dionysius. Pythias asked to be released to travel to see his family to tell them goodbye. He also promised to return in seven days to face his execution. Dionysius did not believe the youth would return and was unwilling to permit the short-term release. However, Damon, a close friend of Pythias, was willing to take his place in prison and said he would also face death in Pythias's place if he did not return in time. Damon told the king, "I am not afraid to take the place of my friend, for he is noble and trustworthy and will return to face his death. Even if he is held by weather or captured by evil men, I am willing to die for a friend as true as Pythias." With this, Dionysius permitted Pythias to leave to say goodbye to his family, and Damon was imprisoned.

The week passed and the guards and king told Damon his friend was not going to return. They said surely he would die in his place. But Damon restated his faith in his friend and his willingness to die if Pythias was killed en route or held by circumstances.

Even the hardhearted king was impressed with Damon and his faithful commitment to his friend.

On the seventh day, Damon was prepared for execution and taken to the prison entrance. As his eyes hit the harsh light from outside the prison, he saw a silhouette. It was his friend Pythias returning. A storm at sea had detained him. Pythias apologized to his friend for his late return and for nearly costing Damon his life. Damon was released and Pythias was bound by the guards.

The crowds had gathered at the place of execution. The king saw the guards pulling their prisoner toward his execution, thinking it was Damon, but then saw it was Pythias. Dionysius was amazed the youth would return, as he had been convinced Pythias would flee and leave Damon to die.

The example of faith and love shown by the two men softened the heart of the tyrant, and he offered Pythias a pardon. Even more, the king asked Damon and Pythias for their friendship so he could learn from them.[4]

This Greek legend of Damon and Pythias is a story retold by Aristoxenus of Tarentum and Marcus Tullius Cicero. It is also used in modern art to provide a story of true friendship. You see, the ancients had a philosophy of friendship and dwelt upon it in their literary works. From the works of Homer, Aristotle, and Cicero we have examples of faith and trust in others and pragmatic steps to identify a true friend.

Jesus also had a philosophy of friendship. (Although many Christians are uncomfortable with the term *philosophy* being applied to Christian ideas, they shouldn't be. In Greek, *philosophy* literally means "love of knowledge.") One could surmise that Jesus loved knowing others—that he loved friends.

As for myself, if not for a friend, I may have never engaged with the ancients. I had read a little of the works of Homer and was familiar only in name with Socrates, Plato, Aristotle, and Seneca, but I had not dug deep into their writings or considered their value in the modern world. Then I met Dr. David Bertch, and his friendship would open countless doors to the past.

---

4   Laban M. T. Hill and James Edward Bates, *The Story of Damon and Pythias* (Victoria, Australia: Leopold Classic Library, 2017).

But I am getting ahead of myself. Before Dr. Bertch, Don Staton became a great influencer in my life. Don and his wife, Helene, taught the young married Sunday school class at our church, Southcliff Baptist Church in Fort Worth. This small group of couples would be a building ground for several lifelong friendships.

Don was in his late sixties when I met him at Southcliff. A good teacher and leader, he put all his efforts into the men and women of our group. He had retired after years of managing his own business.

Don made time for the men in our class. He would meet with us for a weekly book club and connect with us individually at breakfast. He introduced us to books he loved that were designed to support or amplify lessons from the Bible. All the books were modern books reflecting on biblical ideas and theology. In my late twenties, I began reading for pleasure for the first time.

Don created environments for learning and debate. He also set aside time to grow individual connections with each of us. He was a friend, but more importantly, a mentor. For over ten years, he was responsible for pushing me deeper into reading and thought, as well as cultivating my friendships with others through introductions he made. He was like a father to many young men.

In November of 2004, Don passed away. He was at a hospital in south Fort Worth for several days, and we were unable to see him, but through his family he sent us a message before he passed. He told me and the others he mentored, "Carry on!"

For the next two years, the thought of him would bring me to tears. I and others had lost a trusted mentor—an old man who had succeeded in life through his relationships and had given us so much wisdom. As I continued to mourn his loss, I realized I was desperate for another friend who had experienced more of life and could help me on my journey as Don had.

Don had set a great example for my wife and me for a decade, but we took on the responsibility to follow his example somewhat reluctantly. After nearly two years, Danae and I began teaching our own class on Sunday mornings at a different church in Fort Worth—Wedgwood Baptist. Following Don's example, during our time teaching at Wedgwood, we would meet more lifelong friends.

Our class included couples in their thirties, forties, and fifties. I was disappointed we didn't have older folks in the class. I felt those in their sixties and seventies had the most to share. I had not lost a job or a child, been through a divorce, put a kid through college, built investment income, failed in a dramatic way, been married for thirty years, etc. Only someone who has experienced these kinds of things in life can counsel others through them. To get these older voices in our class, I decided I would have to go out and find them. Thus, I put an ad in our weekly church publication:

Dear Old People, we are in desperate need of your experience and wisdom. Our class has no one from sixty to eighty years old and we would like to invite you to join us in fellowship so we might learn from you.

Two weeks later David and Barbara Bertch, in their mid-sixties, walked into our class in response to the posting. After class, Dr. Bertch came up to me and asked, "Do you like to read?" I affirmed I had an interest in books, and he asked me what I was reading. He was not impressed with my list or the authors. He said, "I like to meet with men and talk about old books. If I suggested a book, would you take the time to read it and then you and I get together each week to discuss it?"

I accepted immediately.

He added, "If you are not going to take the time to read, I won't take the time to discuss it. So be prepared, for there is no need for us to waste time."

This man was serious.

"Have you read *Pensées* by Blaise Pascal?" Dr. Bertch asked.

"No, sir; that is unfamiliar to me."

"Let's read a book that talks about the *Pensées*—*Christianity for Modern Pagans*. You buy a copy this week."

And so, we began reading our first book together in the spring of 2006. He would introduce me to Pascal, Aristotle, Boethius, Plato, Dante, Seneca, Xenophon, Cicero, and more.

I had found another friend and mentor. Mentors as friends can certainly enrich our lives, and this is exactly what Don Staton and David Bertch did for me. I know on the surface this sounds simple, but I never would have heard the story of Damon and Pythias if not for my friend Dr. Bertch. The great examples and outlines of friendship from the past would have been lost to me without his influence. We miss so much about life and friendship without the ancients—and it is irrefutable that the ancient is missing in the modern.

The ancient writers and philosophers are now relegated to micro-introductions in middle school and poorly taught Philosophy 101 college courses. They are truly appreciated by only a select few who study the humanities, and that is a shrinking number. Even beyond the ancients, little time is spent with writings from medieval monks, the reformers, the French and American revolutionists, and modern philosophers. The modern world doesn't waste time on authors who don't teach us to conform to job functions or show us how to make money or how to be happy. Yet, if we read those of the past, we would learn how to live well, how to find meaning, and how to live with others.

The modern philosopher tells us, "L'enfer, c'est les autres" (i.e., "Hell is other people")—the famous phrase of Jean-

Paul Sartre.[5] In his play *Huis clos* (*No Exit* in English), Sartre tells us the judgment we receive from others is unimportant, as we are a work in progress. However, it is the input, the judgment of others, that can improve us and move us to a more completed work.

The modern philosopher wants us to be free from judgment and not suffer the anxiety of validation from outside sources. Instead of seeking outside counsel and critique, the modern turns to themselves for validation.

Not the ancient philosophers, however.

An ancient, Aristotle, tells us, "But the good man is to his friend as to himself, friend being but a name for a second Self . . . therefore one ought to be thoroughly more aware of one's own existence."[6] Hell is not other individuals, but in fact, it is heaven if we embrace them fully and remain open to their critiques.

The ancients thought deeply about the idea of friendship. For them, it did not begin and end with someone you could talk with about sports and have a beer. However, this may be an activity within a friendship. The ancients found purpose and meaning in the development of friendships. They defined the different types and identified what they called a "true friend." Let's examine this.

---

5   Jean-Paul Sartre, *Huis clos*, 1st ed. (Upper Saddle River, NJ: Pearson Education Company, 1963), 91.

6   Aristotle, *Nicomachean Ethics*, trans. William D. Ross (CreateSpace Independent Publishing Platform: Scotts Valley, CA, 2016), 299.

Question: Would you take the place of one of your friends if you knew it might mean your death if they did not return? Would you be willing to die even if their intentions were good, but there was the possibility of their ship being destroyed at sea? The example of Damon and Pythias may be extreme, but do you think this deeply about the friendships in your life? Have you pondered what you learn from your friends? Have you thought about what they are learning from you? Have you dwelt upon your example to them and theirs to you? Have you reflected on the life events, simple or dramatic, you've been through together?

I don't expect you to answer all of these questions (right away anyhow), but I do expect you to know this: The ancients can help us develop a philosophy of friendship. Following their example, you can develop a philosophy of friendship to guide you in your relationships with others. Your constructed view of friendship will help you identify who you can serve, where you are lacking, what you can learn from others, and who has the makings of a true friend. The ancients can help you understand where you are in the growth of friendship and what steps you should take to move forward or even retreat from a relationship.

It is so uncanny. I don't find many men thinking deeply about friendship, but if we take the time to understand our philosophy of friendship, we will have an opportunity to improve the lives of those around us and our own. Is this not what this life is about?

Yes, it is true. Some of my friends are dead. They are men of the ancient past whose words were saved in print. As I read their writings, I commune with them. I discover how much we have in common, and I gain wisdom from their contemplations. Come with me, my friends. Follow my example—the same example I have followed: Commune with dead people through their writings. I promise this will lead to an interesting conversation.

Chapter 4

A SECOND SELF

Cicero was a central figure in the story of the Roman Empire. He lived at the crossroads of history and would give voice to a republic. Fearless, he risked his life for the ideas and individuals he believed in, which unfortunately cost him his life. His writings survived him: *On Duties, Treatises on Friendship and Old Age*, and over nine hundred other letters.[7]

Cicero was born in 106 BC to a family of means, who moved to Rome when Cicero was just a child. His education was focused on rhetoric, philosophy, and law; his teachers were prominent men of the age. He began his legal career in his mid-twenties, and before long he had a reputation as a talented and courageous man who uncovered countless acts of corruption. Although he was seen as a savior of the people, his efforts also earned him many enemies.

---

7   Cicero, introductory note in *Treatises on Friendship and Old Age*, trans. E. S. Shuckburgh (New York: Another Leaf Press, 2009).

In 49 BC, as Caesar and Pompey battled, Cicero sided with Pompey. After Caesar had control and Pompey was killed in Egypt, Caesar showed Cicero grace, most likely in recognition of his talent and contributions as a whole.

After Caesar's assassination, Cicero supported the cause of the conspirators against Antony. He had no regard for Antony and his behavior and wrote against him in what are known as the fourteen "Philippics." To ensure the great orator and writer never spoke or wrote again, agents of Antony found him and cut off his head and hands, then displayed them in Rome.

Cicero's writings have stood the test of time and still live two thousand years after his death. The views of this Roman statesman are useful in practical living today as well as for current political comparison. While he had enemies, his service, intelligence, and bravery earned him many friends in Rome.

One of the great lasting works of Cicero is his *Treatises on Friendship and Old Age*—a dialogue between Gaius Laelius and Laelius's two sons-in-law, Gaius Fannius and Quintus Mucius Scaevola. After his friend Scipio's death, Laelius reflects on their friendship with the two young men. Within the work, we are given much to contemplate about identifying those who may make good friends and how we should serve one another.

The first thing Cicero's Laelius provides for us is a view of the nature of their friendship. Consider the words of Laelius:

Such is the pleasure I take in recalling our friendship that I look upon my life as having been a happy one because I spent it with Scipio. With him I was associated in public and private business, with him I lived in Rome and served abroad, and between us there was the most complete harmony in tastes, our pursuits, and our sentiments which is the true secret of friendship.[8]

Thus, Cicero's view of friendship shows accord through like-mindedness. There was a "complete harmony" in what the pair enjoyed, sought, and thought. If we took this short phrase alone, we may very well limit our friends to a select few. If we use this as a measurement, I suggest we use this description for those friends in our innermost circle. Let's define our first group of friends, then, as our inner circle—a circle of complete harmony.

It is difficult to build an inner circle. It takes time and opportunities to trust before we allow someone into such a space. We will have like-minded folks in our inner circle and thus may be able to share things with them that others could take the wrong way. No matter the consequences, however, we allow those in this circle to be close to us, and we desire closeness with them. Cicero takes it further as Laelius also states, "I must begin by laying down this principle—friendship can only exist between good men."[9] He then defines what he means by good:

---

8 Cicero, *Treatises*, 14.
9 Cicero, *Treatises*, 15.

those whose actions and lives leave no question as to their honor, purity, equity, and liberality, who are free from greed, lust, and violence, and who have the courage of their convictions.[10]

Using his definition of good shrinks the field of candidates for our inner circle. We are left with much weighing and measuring of ourselves and those around us. Is he wrong?

If we are to permit people into our inner circle, we must agree with Cicero. If someone is not virtuous, he is likely untrustworthy. Therefore, the friendship may fail. If a virtuous individual offends in the relationship, then at some point he will do the honorable step and ask for forgiveness, a sign of goodness that can put us back in harmony.

The most important reflection from Cicero's expectation of goodness is our self-evaluation. Do we meet his standards? If we discover through honest self-reflection we do not, then we give ourselves things to work on. The most important work we do in friendship is to improve ourselves to better serve others. We now have like-mindedness and goodness, and our guide Laelius adds something more: affection. He says, "You may eliminate affection from relationships, you cannot do so from friendship."[11]

Cicero is courageous, tough, and unwavering. He calls us to affection in true friendship. He calls us to love one another but

---

10   Cicero, *Treatises*, 15.

11   Cicero, *Treatises*, 16.

makes it clear that reciprocal love has expectations. Using Jesus as an example, a Christian may criticize Cicero's expectations that should be met before offering affection, but Jesus and the Bible provide examples of walking away from others, or not offering affection. Some Christians have taken the example from the book of Matthew quite literally:

> "Whatever town or village you enter, search there for some worthy person and stay at their house until you leave. As you enter the home, give it your greeting. If the home is deserving, let your peace rest on it; if it is not, let your peace return to you. If anyone will not welcome you or listen to your words, leave that home or town and shake the dust off your feet. Truly I tell you, it will be more bearable for Sodom and Gomorrah on the day of judgment than for that town." (Matthew 10:11–15)

I don't think most Christians today would see this as a pattern for friendship. I won't expound on it, but I believe Jesus was making a point about eternity, not about how we should engage with others. But let us not forget Jesus has expectations of our friendship with him: He calls us to love God and love one another. Love or affection "covers a multitude of sins" (1 Peter 4:8). This love spoken of by the apostle Peter describes love among an inner circle of friends or, as it is called in Christianity, a local body of believers.

Jesus calls Christians to "love your neighbor as yourself" (Matthew 22:39). Cicero—and before him, Aristotle— called us to the same action hundreds of years before Christ, but not in the broad sense Jesus is using. If you recall, Aristotle calls a friend a "second self." Cicero uses this same term in his *Treatises*:

> In the face of a true friend a man sees a second self. So that where his friend is he is; if his friend be rich, he is not poor, though he be weak, his friend's strength is his. Such friendship enhances prosperity and relieves adversity of its burden by halving and sharing it.[12]

Plus, in true friendship, Cicero defines motive: affection.

> I gather that friendship springs from a natural impulse rather than a wish for help: from an inclination of the heart, combined with a certain instinctive feeling of love, rather than from a calculation of the material advantage it is likely to confer.[13]

According to Cicero, this "instinctive feeling of love" comes from goodness, from virtuousness. "Nothing conciliates affection like virtue," he writes.[14] What this means for us is that within our inner circle, we must be virtuous. Those we permit into this closeness must also display goodness. Finally, this mutual goodness becomes a source of our affection.

As stated earlier, in our friendships we must spend time in self-reflection to ensure we are bringing goodness and affection to

---

12   Cicero, *Treatises*, 17.
13   Cicero, *Treatises*, 19.
14   Cicero, *Treatises*, 19.

the relationship. Our lives must be put together if we are to offer service and affection to another. In describing someone ready to develop friendships, Cicero writes,

> He is so fortified by virtue and wisdom as to want nothing and to feel absolutely self-dependent, it is then that he is most conspicuous for seeking out and keeping friendships.[15]

In Christianity, we can again layer the statement of Jesus, "Love your neighbor as yourself" (Matthew 22:39). How can you be an affectionate, true friend if you are not virtuous, thoughtful, and open to affection? Although it may seem selfish, self-reflection and self-correction are truly ways of loving yourself and preparing yourself to be affectionate toward others. Love yourself enough to "fortify virtue and wisdom" so you might be virtuous toward another. In doing so, you set an example of being a true friend and give yourself the potential to gain a true friend.

An unvirtuous person may have relationships but risks never having a true friend—or an inner circle for that matter. And in friendship, unvirtuous behavior may destroy the connection. "Friendship can hardly remain if virtue be abandoned," Laelius warns.[16] I must point out that although we may have different definitions of virtue, the ancients used the term to convey excellence. They defined the main virtues as courage, moderation, justice, and piety. It is important to reflect on your

---

15 Cicero, *Treatises*, 20.
16 Cicero, *Treatises*, 23.

definitions of *virtue*, as this is vital for being in a relationship with a "second self."

In defining virtue, we run into a modern conundrum. *Truth* is now degraded to "my truth," a phrase of the current culture. No longer are there global, national, or corporate agreements of what is true and virtuous. The particulars and measurements now flow solely to individual choices and inconsistencies. The current culture would have you seek your feelings, follow your heart, or do what you think is right. We are not pushed to challenge our thoughts, feelings, and actions to consider where our desires and impulses may negatively impact our lives or the lives of others. Society says, "If it feels good, do it!" No longer do we lean on universal agreements.

I hesitate to say you need to define what you believe to be virtuous—I am more inclined to tell you to seek what is virtuous and true. Your search should begin with the tenants of faith and the thoughts of the ancients.

The ancient stoics and Christians provide the clearest picture of virtuous character and action to build upon.

If we have a definition and understanding of goodness, then we will operate best in friendships where the understanding and actions of goodness are shared.

The way we define goodness will define whom we welcome into our inner circle and who will welcome us into theirs. Our true friends, our "second selves," are the relationships we most crave in life. The closeness and affection of such relationships give life meaning and purpose. To serve someone is to give value to his life. To pursue someone is to give meaning to your life. The other side of the same coin has to do with a friend's absence. Thus, to lose someone is to understand in full the value he had brought to your life. For me, the deaths of David Rutherford and Don Staton were painful because these true friends had added so much value to my life. My reflection then turns to, "If I had died first, would they have felt the same pain?"

Let us explore more considerations to help you prepare yourself to be "fortified in virtue and wisdom."[17]

17   Cicero, *Treatises*, 20.

Chapter 5

AFRAID OF THE QUIET

L IFE OFFERS CONTINUOUS LESSONS. The sincere learner welcomes both the negative and the positive until his final moment on the planet. Our past and present friendships can and should be building our character at every turn. Friendships—both successful and unsuccessful—should bring reflection. I have experienced failed friendships where the responsibility for the failure fell on me—my actions or lack thereof. At the same time, there are friendships I ended abruptly because of things I began recognizing about the other person. Whatever the case may be, if we are intentionally pursuing others, we will have many different experiences. Consequently, we must be introspective throughout these relationships.

Introspection should be our first step in serving others and a process we must return to with great frequency. This is how we achieve Cicero's directive to be "fortified in virtue and wisdom."[18] It can be said the best friends to be and have are those who are lifelong learners. To shed some light on this, let us begin by defining some ways we can search our souls and improve the development of friendships in our lives.

Do you love yourself? I was told when I was single if I was unhappy as a single person, I would be even unhappier when I married. The warning I received was to never go into marriage thinking another person would be able to solve my problems.

Another individual is never responsible for making you feel a certain way. You are responsible for your attitude and response to the events around you. A spouse is not there to solve your relationship issues at work, keep you from feelings of depression or disconnection, or make you feel needed or important. A good wife will attempt to help you, but it is not her assignment to solve your problems.

Marriage is for two people who have discovered themselves as individuals and were content to be alone before marriage. In getting to know each other, both discover their love of the other person and want nothing more than to love and serve each other. If an individual comes to the marriage *expecting* the other person to meet their needs, improve their self-esteem, or bring them joy, the marriage is in trouble from the start.

An over-dependence on your wife will create stresses on the relationship. Leaning on her to be the solution or escape

---

18   Cicero, *Treatises on Friendship and Old Age*, trans. E. S. Shuckburgh (New York: Another Leaf Press, 2009), 20.

from your problems asks too much of her. There are several reasons for this.

First, you may be asking too much of her time and not providing the space for her to pursue what she enjoys.

Second, over-dependence with no improvement may cause undue stress. You may be frustrated when you begin to doubt her ability to change or help you.

Third, expecting your wife to be the solution may give her concerns of your ability to contribute to the relationship and a fear about what the future may hold for the two of you.

A marriage relationship offers a great gift: the opportunity to serve the other person in love and support. It is also the responsibility of each not to burden the other with issues and events they cannot solve.

Sharing your feelings and experiences with your wife is of paramount importance—be sure to include thoughts about how you are managing or pursuing resolutions to your own challenges.

In times of sadness or depression, I've shared with my wife my emotions and the events, memories, or fears that led to what I was experiencing. It was never her responsibility to make me happy or experience joy. I always let her know this was my responsibility, and I often solved issues by going away alone for a weekend of hiking to think and pray. I shared my experience but kept the responsibility of solutions.

We are ready for marriage and to serve another only when we have our own life in order. Then we will have a healthy understanding of ourselves, self-discovered joys, and self-love. This may sound selfish, but it is not. Obviously, when we do this, we are not narcissists, but individuals who can move through life in healthy relationships because we have much more to give than to take.

Friendship is no different. You have the makings for being a good friend to someone else if you have spent the time and reflection to understand yourself and to find joy in life without depending on others. This is not to say we are not all dependent on one another, nor is it to say there is not joy in being with others. However, it *is* to say your joy does not depend on others and their actions. You must dig deep for these types of inner virtues.

The only way we can fortify ourselves in virtue is to take time to reflect and meditate. We must be willing to ask ourselves hard questions, find the answers, and respond to our discoveries without distractions. In our busy lives, few men make time for such reflection. Even more so, most men don't want to acknowledge their own weaknesses or to have to change themselves. That would mean admitting to something being wrong; hence, it is easier to avoid challenges, changes, and problems.

Taking the time to sit quietly and reflect is something people have avoided for centuries. Blaise Pascal wrote about the problem in the seventeenth century. He was amazed at how busy and occupied people were in the mid-1600s. This passage included in his *Pensées* remains true: "All of humanity's problems stem from man's inability to sit quietly in a room alone."[19] Thus, we've been aware of this problem for centuries. So, why are we as men so complacent?

If you are serious about fortifying virtue, caring for others, producing something good in the world, or finding God, you must make time to be alone, read, meditate, reflect, and discern. This process will permit you to understand and define yourself, your beliefs, your failures, your motives, and your goals.

One way to accomplish this is by taking a sabbatical. (I can hear it now: Who's got time for that? Right?) A sabbatical doesn't have to last for weeks, months, or years—it can be useful even if it is just a weekend. A couple of days away from our daily duties and familiar places can offer the solitude and quiet we need to reflect.

I was in my forties when I took my first sabbatical weekend. My friend David Bertch had given me the book *Consolation of Philosophy* by Boethius. I wanted the time to read it with intent and consider its application. After leaving work on a Friday afternoon, I drove up to an old state park hotel at Lake Murray in Oklahoma. I checked in to my room and started reading— and continued reading until late in the evening. I woke early and went for a quiet walk around the lake, then returned to my room to read. It rained most of the day, and the sound of the

---

19   Blaise Pascal, "Pensées," section 139, in *Pensées and Other Writings*, trans. Honor Levi (Oxford: Oxford University Press, 1995).

falling rain was perfect for reading and meditating. The quiet permitted the powerful lines of ancient text to jump from the page deep into my soul. I felt truly fortified. Let me explain. . . .

Boethius shares a vision of philosophy as a woman coming to him in his prison cell to console him and elevate his understanding of his difficult situation. So, here is this man Boethius at the lowest point in his life after living a life of means and great authority. He is falsely accused of treason against the king of the Ostrogoths. King Theodoric sentenced Boethius to torture and death. Times were hard, but Boethius used philosophy to ask the right questions in order to work through his situation, his life, and his purpose.

I love to think about Boethius sitting quietly, working through the tough questions. Eleven hundred years before Pascal, Boethius was showing us how to sit quietly and ask ourselves difficult questions.

As Boethius sits in his cell, the woman asks him to answer questions such as these:

> "What is the source of your sadness?" "Have you forgotten what you are capable of?" "Are you relying on external things such as wealth and power to bring you happiness?" "Have you lost sight of the ultimate goal in life to seek the good and the true?"[20]

---

20 Boethius, *Consolation of Philosophy*, trans. Victor Watts (London: Penguin Classics, 1999), bk. II, prose IV, 61.

Boethius, one of the last ancient philosophers, would have us follow the advice of Cicero. Here are Boethius's last written words to us before his death:

> Avoid vice therefore and cultivate virtues; lift up your mind to the right kind of hope and put forth humble prayers on high. A great necessity is laid upon you, if you will be honest with yourself, a great necessity to do good, since you live in the sight of a judge who sees all things.[21]

In Boethius's last hours he was still attempting to improve himself and his understanding of the world. His fire for inner virtue never went out.

In their thoughtful moments, the ancients are calling us to a virtuous life. In our quiet moments, we may consider our character, past and present, with a desire to cultivate better patterns for the future. Because this type of reflection seldom happens in the busyness of life, time for reflection must be scheduled into our lives to care for ourselves and to prepare us for the care of others. As we begin this process of reflection, what questions can we ask ourselves?

Here are a few to get you started: What are your motives in your relationships with others? In the relationships you currently enjoy, are you meeting their needs more than they are meeting yours? Are you in the relationship solely because of what you receive from them?

---

21   Boethius, *Consolation of Philosophy*, bk. V, prose VI, 169.

Keep in mind, we may benefit in many ways from our relationships, but the motive in the pursuit of others should be how we might improve their lives and how we respond virtuously in our relationship to them. There are plenty of unvirtuous motives in the pursuit of others—one of the most common is personal gain.

If we reflect on our lives and our motives, we should also reflect on our means. The methods we use to reach and interact with others are important and differ by individual. Knowing what you love and enjoy provides ways for you to develop relationships. Whether through sports, books, games, work, hobbies, religion, politics, or passions, you can use these as methods of introduction and interaction.

David Bertch and I built our friendship from a love of reading and talking about books. My friendship with John Pribble grew from hiking and climbing together. My relationship with Darrin Kirby deepened from working closely together. My friendships with Monty Jones, Richard Sammons, and Britt Lane resulted from church discussions about religious ideas. All the things we enjoy in life can be mediums for meeting and growing relationships. If you can't make a solid list of the things you love, you need to try new things.

After you reflect on your lives, motives, and means, you should reflect on your purpose. What is the most important thing in your life that you want others to know or understand? What difficult experience in your life has prepared you to help someone in a similar situation? What's something new you can introduce others to, something you love and are familiar with? What are the hopes and desires of those around you? Can you help them reach their goals?

As we sit quietly and reflect, we can also weigh and measure our past and current friendships and the impact the other person may have on us. Some of the relationships we call "friendships" may in fact be bad for us, but, for now, just know the intentional pursuit of others begins with and requires continued reflection. Indeed, the greatest activity we can bring to our relationships with others is taking the time to be alone and to thoughtfully consider our lives, our relationships, and our contributions to others. Only this can prepare us for true friendship in the way Boethius described it: "the most precious of all riches—friends who are true friends."[22]

---

22   Boethius, *Consolation of Philosophy*, bk. II, prose VIII, 77.

Chapter 6

AN INVITATION TO ADVENTURE

Pamplona is not a city for old men, but at six in the morning, the streets were full of men and women of all ages sleeping on the patches of grass as well as on the doorsteps. The festival's first day was full of dancing and drinking. Many young people could not find a hotel to stay in for the night. We were up early to find a good spot for the morning's festivities, which were to begin promptly at eight o'clock.

The night before, we had enjoyed a great dinner but decided to stay away from cocktails and wine so we would be as alert as possible for the next morning. As we made our way through the crowd, it was clear we were some of the few sober people. We were also some of the oldest. My companions and I were in our forties, but the men crowding in around us looked to be mostly in their mid-twenties.

We stood in the city's iconic city center as music began to ring out from various streets. Men waved rolled-up newspapers in the air and passed around their wineskins full of sangria. We found ourselves in an Australian contingency, and the boys, standing six-foot-plus, shouted for us to open our mouths so they could pour the sangria into them and celebrate with us.

We were incredibly excited, but underlying the energy and zeal of the moment lived a suppressed fear. We shuffled past dead man's curve, as we had seen the carnage from historic videos, and we made our way on to the straightaway, which led to the Coliseum.

We heard the boom of the rocket and knew the movement had arrived. There was no turning back. The crowds surged and the roars grew. I lost track of my friends. It was now every man for himself.

I looked ahead. About a hundred yards away, I saw the bouncing of the horns. The bulls and steers had made their way onto Calle Estafeta. I started to pray but then stopped. *Why would God listen to a fool?* Then, I ran. Seconds passed, but there I was running at arm's length with the fearsome bulls on the streets of Pamplona. I was yelling, shoving men who stopped in front of me to the ground, and hoping I did not make a wrong step or turn.

Unbeknownst to me, a couple of steers ran farther behind the main group of bulls, which made it possible for me to race into the Coliseum right behind the bulls. I gave it my all, but when I looked up, I was standing in the middle of the famous bullring of Hemingway fame. I was singing, "¡Olé! ¡Olé!" and then saw the face of my close friend Darrin Kirby. Darrin and I were in disbelief but thrilled to be uninjured. All the pent-up fear turned into elation and celebration.

"We're alive!" Darrin yelled over the crowd. "We're alive!"

"I just ran," I yelled back. "I was going to pray, but I figured God thought I was being foolish!"

Then Darrin yelled, "Run!"

Just then a bull was released back out into the arena. Our little fiesta ended as we scattered in different directions like frightened fish escaping from a dolphin. Several bulls were rereleased, which entertained the crowd in the seats as they screamed with joy with every close call in the ring.

Twenty minutes later, we all found our way out of the arena and back to our families, who were watching the events from a balcony along the run.

Our Running of the Bulls in the San Fermin Festival in 2011 was the fulfillment of a dream and an adventure of a lifetime for us. The event and the surrounding days solidified a great friendship between Darrin and me for eternity. Nothing strengthens friendship like a shared adventure. The bigger the experience, the more dangerous, the more strenuous, the more unpredictable, the more it brings you together. At least, this has been my experience. Let me explain. . . .

Darrin and I shared an experience few people understand but almost everyone is familiar with. Each year from July 6 to 14, the world turns an eye to Pamplona: the chaos of thousands of men in white and red running through ancient streets with bulls bred to kill. And while the world is familiar with the event, Darrin and I understand the fear, know the smell, have run the streets, and lived to tell the tale. When we are with others, we share in telling the story and relive it over and over. Adventure binds friends close. Remember, men tend to live pretty boring—yet busy—lives these days. They go to work and stay indoors most of the time. For this very reason, most men are looking for—if not longing for—an outdoor adventure.

Most guys are more than ready to accept an invitation to adventure. Consequently, creating an adventure and inviting people to come along is a powerful way to pursue people for friendship. Plus, there is something about the outdoors that helps men tap into their primal selves and fosters lasting—not just casual—relationships. Pope John Paul II, for example, knew all about this.

Pope John Paul II enjoyed skiing, hiking, and kayaking. His love of the outdoors is well documented. As a young man in Poland, he had a hard time getting men to come to mass. The liturgical service bored many, as it was unfamiliar and not fully understood. In an effort to build connections, John Paul began inviting men to go on hikes with him. While they were hiking, he would talk about the things they wanted to discuss, and he would share about his faith and church. Through these small adventures, John Paul developed connections with others as he introduced them to what he saw as the most important thing in life, a relationship with God. Adventure opened the door.

I shared about The May Club, which I co-founded with David Rutherford. Each year we plan a different location. In 2016, I was with about six other guys on a trip to Arches National Park. We had decided to do the five-mile round trip hike of Devil's Garden. I had done this hike years before when it was 107 degrees and did not take enough water. Let me tell you the truth: This was maybe the closest I've come to heatstroke. However, during our 2016 hike, the weather was cooler, and storms were in the forecast. Our group included some veteran outdoorsmen and a few gentlemen who did not hike very often.

The storms came and began to pelt us with hail. We found some rocks to hide under. As the hail stopped, we continued our hike, but the lightning was fast approaching. Michael Scott was one of the men on the hike, and he was counting the time from the lightning to the clap of thunder. He simply warned, "It's getting closer."

It turns out rocks are not exactly a great escape from lightning, and we were at the bottom of the trail. The rain was now pouring down, and the lighting had us ducking with every flash. The water began to rise, and a flash flood filled the trails and poured off the surrounding rock formations. We came to an area of slick rock, and the entire trail where we needed to hike was now waist deep or more.

In order to ford the slick rocks, we formed a human chain. It was impossible for some to get a grip on the rock with their shoes. The next rock feature would prove even more dangerous in the rain, especially for those with the wrong shoes. With the limited grip, slick stone, and long drop, one by one, we hung on to each other to keep anyone from falling.

The last mile was nothing but sand—about a four-hundred-foot ascent. The storm had passed, and temperatures rose quickly. Trudging through that sand wore everyone out.

And yet . . . Moab was the greatest hike I've ever experienced. The weather was horrible and there was a risk, but I made it through with Wes, Charles, Michael, Larry, Trevor, Darrin, Terry, Saul, John, Patrick, and Cliff. It became a more aggrandized story over the years, but it was a moment shared with friends and a lifelong connection through adventure.

As I meet people through work, church, and my neighborhood, I sometimes invite men to join us. I often tell stories about adventures with The May Club. If someone says they would enjoy something like it, I give them an invite. These invitations are a win-win. Let me explain. . . .

First, I've discovered people appreciate an invitation, even if they do not accept. We all want to be included, and an invitation to a trip, event, or party is a sign of being appreciated. It's a big, lonely world, and to be included can change a person.

Just a call, an email, or a text inviting someone to be a part of an event or adventure may be a lifesaving step. Your interest in another may save them from loneliness or despair. A simple invitation lets others know they are thought about. It's a gift to be thought of and considered.

Second, there are not a lot of relationship building events going on for middle-aged men. There are plenty of kid games, school functions, and block parties, but not adventurous opportunities. Whether or not men know how to hunt, fish, climb, or kayak, they always appreciate an invitation to go hang out with the guys.

Here is how I see it: An invitation is a starting point in the pursuit of others that could lead to an adventure. However, without an invitation, there will be no event to build common ground on. Hence, an invitation is needed to achieve the goal of connecting with people in a real way. Everything must start somewhere, and an invitation is the cornerstone of friendship. Likewise, the conversations that happen during the process of travel and adventure are the building blocks of friendship.

These adventure-time dialogues are catalysts for long-term connections to build—more so when you discover a shared interest or struggle. C. S. Lewis says it best in his book *The Four Loves*:

> Friendship arises out of mere companionship when two or more of the companions discover that they have in common some insight or interest or even taste which the others do not share and which, till that moment, each believed to be his own unique treasure (or burden). The typical expression

of opening Friendship would be something like, "What? You too? I thought I was the only one." . . . It is when two such persons discover one another, when, whether with immense difficulties and semi-articulate fumblings or with what would seem to us amazing and elliptical speed, they share their vision—it is then that Friendship is born. And instantly they stand together in an immense solitude.[23]

Being alone together against the world! That is what it is all about! I've straddled a rattlesnake in a slot canyon with my buddies. Climbing at 13,500 feet, I've sat with my arm around a friend in an attempt to warm up in a blizzard. I've kayaked in the gulf thinking lightning would get us before we made it back to shore. All great events because they ended well, but greater events because of the conversations that took place during a shared experience.

Conversations can start simply with questions. And sure, you can start a conversation by inviting someone on an adventure, but also invite them into a conversation. For example, my friend Clint Woodward is a pro at getting people to talk. He has a gift for that, and he taught it to me over the years. You notice three very interesting things whenever you watch Clint engage with another person.

First, he is always asking about them, opening the door for them to share. Clint seldom talks about himself unless asked. Second, as he asks questions, he is actively listening. I am

23 C. S. Lewis, *The Four Loves* (New York: Harcourt Brace Jovanovich Publishers, 1960), 96.

amazed at all he can retain from a conversation, but this is because he asks questions with a sincere interest in the other person. Last, he serves the person during the conversation. He'll get up and grab him another beer, fill up his drink, and ask him if he needs anything or wants to take a break. He is asking, listening, and serving. That is how it is done.

I enjoy listening to and serving others. Let's go back to the best example I have: I have been inviting people for adventures for three decades. I have planned the annual May Club trip and an annual May Club Die-Hard trip for the more adventurous . . . father-daughter camping trips and father-son trips . . . and a few large dinner events with the guys each year. I am excited when people in my various circles have asked about The May Club out of genuine shock that such a group exists without connection to a club or church. They are often surprised when I share these are just people I've met throughout my life and invited to join me. Then I ask them, "Do you want to go?"

It all begins with an ask. That is the starting point, but remember also that adventure does not have to be learning to jump out of an airplane or sledding down Everest. Although this would be a perfectly fine invitation, an adventure can be an hour-long hike just outside of town, or a shoreline fishing day, or a paddle around a local lake. Sometimes the simpler, the better. The idea is to get outdoors alone with someone in order to get outside of yourselves. This simple invitation can lead to great conversations and lifelong friendships. An invitation to adventure is an invitation to friendship.

Chapter 7

THE PRIMARY PATH

Not much is known about Aristotle. Many of his writings did not survive, as they were never meant for publication. We do know Aristotle was a student of Plato, and Plato was a student of Socrates. We also know Aristotle at one time tutored Alexander the Great. His writings that did survive influenced the early Middle Ages, as well as the Renaissance. His influence is felt in Judeo and Islamic philosophies. Thomas Aquinas in the thirteenth century forever sealed Aristotle's influence in Catholicism.

Aristotle dealt with a variety of subjects in his writings, including friendship. The depths we could go into with Aristotle are as deep as the ocean floor, so we'll skim the surface of his friendship philosophy. In fact, something I find most intriguing is one Cicero built from Aristotle, who walked the planet nearly three hundred years prior. Aristotle called true friendship "primary friendship" and expanded the category of friends further.[24]

Aristotle defines the relationship between two virtuous individuals as primary friendship. If we review his definitions, we will find unity between his writings and those of Cicero. However, Aristotle expands our categories of friendship beyond primary to friendships of utility and pleasure. Consequently, these types of friendships would be familiar to you as a modern man. Often friendships at work are for the purpose of moving the company forward and creating a harmonious work environment, purely for utility. And there are men in our lives we would not share our deep thoughts with, but we enjoy their company over drinks or like what the connection with them gives us access to.

We might file friendships of utility and pleasure under associate or acquaintance. Aristotle and Cicero both understood these types of relationships, but for both, they lacked affection and tended to be temporal.

Author Suzanne Stern-Gillet writes about the subcategories of friendship in her book *Aristotle's Philosophy of Friendship*:

> Friendships of utility and pleasure can be compared to processes. Being essentially instrumental, friendships of utility not infrequently fade out once their goal has been achieved, and their desirability depends on that of the ends

---

24   Aristotle, quoted in Suzanne Stern-Gillet, *Aristotle's Philosophy of Friendship* (Albany: State University of New York Press, 1995), 37.

they serve . . . at the mercy of the partners' superficial and changing interests or tastes, and as such, they are prone to ebb away whenever they cease to be a source of entertainment or diversion for them.[25]

A friendship of utility or pleasure is not built by providing good for the other. It comes from a selfishness, from wanting to use the other person. In these relationships, we lack trust and affection and may not see the other person as a second self.

Stern-Gillet writes, "In perfect friendship, he [Aristotle] indicates each partner makes the other the ends of his activities as a friend, and any benefit that he himself stands to derive from the association is incidental to his motivation."[26]

Our first motivations are to be the needs of our friend and not the benefits of their company or influence we may seek to gain or use. The benefits are secondary gifts—not profit to be sought.

Can every relationship you have become a primary or true friend? No. Not every association will grow into the goal of true friendship. You've met many a person you would not deem virtuous. You may even know or have known some people with evil motivations. Then you may be drawn to certain people who reject a deeper friendship or may be mentally incapable of such. There are myriad reasons someone may not become a

---

25   Stern-Gillet, *Aristotle's Philosophy of Friendship*, 43.
26   Stern-Gillet, *Aristotle's Philosophy of Friendship*, 65.

primary friend, but any past negative experiences should not deter you from seeking out true friends.

Aside from primary friendships, I would imagine you have not sat down and defined the different relationships in your life. Consider this your call to do so. Defining the relationships in your life takes you another step closer to the intentional pursuit of others. There are probably a lot of different relationships for you to consider: your family, neighbors, coworkers, clients, and social circles. This is not going to be an easy task. Before starting, you need to define your purpose and develop some categories where you place your current relationships.

First, your goal should be to find examples of true friendship—people you are affectionate toward because you see them as a second self. People you serve simply because of who they are. You want to see them thrive and succeed. You want them to know there is someone who cares about them, supports them, and is available to them in meeting their needs.

The path to primary friendships will be full of secondary and tertiary relationships as well. In your life, you will encounter countless numbers of individuals who will never be in your inner circle, but if you are seeking true friendship, you can live with sincerity in all your connections. That is, strive to always be a virtuous person and to attract other virtuous individuals through your actions. Determine to understand the dynamics and purposes of utility and pleasure relationships and to choose not to abuse or take advantage of others.

We never know when an encounter can grow into a deeper relationship. For example, if we are unkind, demanding, or dismissive with the waiter at our table—a chance encounter when out for dinner—we might miss an opportunity to discover a true friend. Who wants to befriend a demanding person or a stingy tipper? Thus, we must begin every chance encounter with kindness and grace, believing the best about someone we know nothing about.

Offer kindness and interest even in the small ways you attempt to meet a need in others' lives. It can be as simple as a greeting or showing gratitude. As you seek true friendship in your life, always interact with others in a way that shows them more valuable than you.

Ungrateful, demanding, arrogant, expectant, dismissive, lording individuals will miss the opportunity to experience true friendship in their lives. Their connections will always be utility and pleasure. Narcissists will believe their relationships are deep, but they will not grasp the reality. The object of their utility or pleasure will use them in the same way and will be waiting for the moment when there is no longer a connection, because the other party knows the narcissist is not virtuous. If you exhibit these traits, it's time for the reflection we spoke of in an earlier chapter. (However, if this is the case, you likely wouldn't be reading this book anyway.)

If you approach all interactions in your life with sincerity, you widen the path to true friendship. This is true in your everyday life. Aristotle introduces us to the farming grounds of friendship, where we must remain sincere in order to have potential friendships. If at work, church, your children's school events, a neighbor's home, or sitting in a bar with people on Thursday nights, you have the opportunity for discovery in your utility and pleasure connections. As long as you are open and honest and sincere, these types of relationships have the potential to turn into true friendships, but they can also be fleeting, not a fulfilling part of life. This does not mean they are unimportant but are simply associations not worthy of being called friendship. These connections are simply friendly with the hope they may grow into friendship.

Furthermore, you do not have a true friendship with your 1,276 "friends" on Facebook, Instagram, LinkedIn, Snapchat, etc. But you do have a farming ground as long as you are sincere in your dealings. Social media is now another part of your life where you must show sincerity. If you are aggressive and unkind in your posts, you have much reflection to do, as such behavior will close the door to true friendship.

If you will consider the pursuit of others as noble, you can find purpose in your casual, utility, and pleasure connections and elevate them beyond trivial interactions.

If you are an individual concerned about the welfare of others, you can define how to sincerely approach initial relationships and take actions that may grow these casual connections into true friends.

Let us continue widening the path to true friendship by looking at categories and definitions of friendship, but doing so with true sincerity.

Chapter 8

CASUAL CONNECTIVITY

ONE OF THE JOYS OF MY LIFE IS BREAKING BREAD WITH PEOPLE FROM ALL OVER THE WORLD—OFTEN IN THEIR LOCAL COMMUNITIES. I've broken Ramadan fast with a family in a Pakistani home, enjoyed chicken from the backyard with a Honduran family in San Pedro Sula, dined on raclette in the French countryside with friends, enjoyed fresh fruit and bread in a small town outside Nuremberg with a close friend and local B&B owners, and eaten stovies with friends and a guide at a local bar after a climb of Ben Nevis in Scotland. What a privilege to meet people and get a glimpse into their daily lives.

When guests visit Fort Worth, I enjoy taking them to a restaurant called Del Frisco's Double Eagle Steak House. For a long time, there were only two locations: one in Dallas and one in Fort Worth. They later expanded across the country, but if you want a steak like the one you make for yourself, their restaurant in Fort Worth is the place to go.

I decided to give an associate visiting town the full Fort Worth stockyards and steak experience. When we arrived, I was greeted by familiar faces, as I often brought clients to the restaurant. When I sat down, a Diet Coke and a Salty Dog were waiting for me; the sommelier was already visiting the table and telling me about a particular wine he had from Ribera Del Duero, a favorite region of mine in Spain. As the restaurant staff offered their greetings and suggestions to me, they were also engaging with my guest, who remained indifferent to all of them. He demanded items, never said thank you, never shook hands with the staff, and never looked up at them. By the end of the evening, he had managed to send his steak back, complain about the food, and never once thank an individual for their time or efforts. I was embarrassed and astonished. I even called the two gentlemen I interacted with at the restaurant to apologize for my guest's behavior and assured them I would never bring him back.

Let's say hypothetically the food was bad this night, or the service was off. This individual was old enough and experienced enough to identify my relationship with the people at the restaurant, and this alone should have warranted a kinder, gentler response in respect of my relationships. Instead, the entire evening was full of disdain, expectancy, and complaint.

For me, this is a rare experience, but for waitstaff around the globe, it is a daily experience. Every day endless numbers of jackasses (i.e., bitter, angry narcissists) walk into places of business with no regard for the individuals serving them. And on some occasions, vice-versa. These encounters are important. In fact, our brief brushes with others are where souls, friendships, and wars are won and lost.

If our aim is true friendship, that begins in the casual conversations and interactions we have with strangers or those we see only every so often. This would seem a simple concept that everyone would grasp, but somehow, we manage to fail on occasion to be kind.

A friendship must have a start. There must be a moment of introduction. A virtuous person will ensure all first encounters are made with a desire to elevate the other individual. Look at it like this. The waiter is not our servant, the doorman is not a doormat, the lady managing the fast-food window is not to be yelled at, and the person cleaning our building is not our personal maid. If we look at people as below us or are unkind because of position or, God forbid, race, creed, sex, or dress, we have made ourselves sons of hell.

The ground is level at the foot of the cross, my friends. A person's career choice or position in life may have nothing to do with his virtuosity. There are incredibly financially successful people without virtue and virtuous individuals who are beginning a career, changing careers, or content in roles you may deem inferior. Put simply, everyone you meet is going through something, so don't judge. If you don't practice virtue, you will never get the opportunity to know them.

Moreover, you will never be close friends with most of the people you meet, but you can behave as if it were possible.

Every meeting could grow into friendship. Being kind helps, but what actions should you take beyond that?

Engage.

With all your interactions, keep the eyes of your heart wide open. Greet and smile when you encounter others. Pay attention to their body language and verbal cues, and respond kindly. Remain open (beyond niceties) to conversations. Ask questions when appropriate, and seek to turn negative situations into positive solutions. Keep your eyes and hearts open. Indeed, this is true engagement.

You should not only keep the eyes of your heart wide open with each interaction but also place others in a position of respect. Show honor to other people, especially those who serve you. Never behave in a way that is haughty or demeaning. Never demand; instead, ask. And most importantly, continuously and endlessly speak and show gratitude. Let me tell you a little story to back this up. . . .

When I was thirty-three years old, I had reached 215 pounds. For a five-foot-six-inch individual, that is way overweight. A friend at work and I decided to get serious about our diet and exercise. Almost every day for months, we went to Applebee's by our office and had salads and hamburgers without a bun. A guy working the lunch hour every day became our regular waiter. When we arrived, he knew exactly what we would be having. And, of course, seeing him almost daily, we began to learn more and more about Myk.

Myk was kind and attentive to us when we were in the restaurant. Over a couple of years, we would see him get married and have a couple of kids. Each interaction led to more and more conversation and life updates. We invited him to join us for The May Club, and he did attend years after we met and continued to attend over the years. My point is this: The casual encounter with Myk—a waiter—led to a true friendship. If we had been closed to connecting on a casual level or expanding casual interactions, we would have missed a great relationship. Myk is my friend, and this is meaningful.

The thing is, it is easy to be dismissive of casual interactions. If you are headed to a business meeting, you may walk into the front lobby and greet the receptionist to advise him or her of a meeting you have with someone. If you sit and wait quietly for your meeting without engaging with the person at the front desk, you are failing to interact with someone who may hold the keys to the company. A person who knows the habits of a client, the likes and dislikes, and the way a system works could give you vital information. You should never be dismissive of a gatekeeper.

Many receptionists have been key to a successful relationship with various business partners I have had, and many also became trusted acquaintances. For example, I've worked for Al Boenker for over twenty-four years. He owns an insurance group in Texas. Al taught me early in my career to "do for those no one else does anything for." He encouraged me to identify people in organizations who carry much of the responsibility and influence but may not be recognized for their efforts. He told me to do this for the business reasons of gaining influence, but more importantly, he said it was because these unnoticed individuals deserve to be recognized. Every person deserves to be seen, thanked, and awarded.

Again, if you allow yourself to be kind and engaging, you may discover the most virtuous and interesting individuals. On the other hand, if you are dismissive of others based on where and how you encounter them, you lose out. Trust me, if your friends believe they deserve to go to the front of the line because of their achievements or background, or if they treat others who serve them poorly, you have unvirtuous friends. If this is your behavior, you need to change.

I've come to believe our behavior in casual encounters may be the greatest measure of our lives. It is in those moments we take for granted that our masks come off and our true selves are revealed. If we work hard enough on what's inside our hearts and become better, more virtuous people, we easily learn to engage others. Finally, people who sincerely want to pursue friendship in their lives develop the virtues of kindness and gratitude.

Chapter 9

WORK ASSOCIATES— GOING BEYOND UTILITY

F RIENDSHIPS AT WORK: IT'S COMPLICATED. It's true that you may find some of the most difficult relationships to manage are in the realm of your work. There are people you report to, people who report to you, clients, vendors, and a world of different personalities you must manage. People are moving through their careers with their own agendas, and often you may encounter untrustworthy individuals and certainly many unvirtuous people. It's easy for your good intentions to be misconstrued. Furthermore, because this is your livelihood, emotions often run high. Befriending those who report to you can create very rough waters, and it takes incredibly mature individuals to successfully navigate these types of relationships. Let's examine this closely.

If you spend eight to ten hours a day with a group of people, you want to do all you can to create a positive atmosphere and good working relationships. As you consider the management of this environment, you should—as always—take the path of serving and elevating others, no matter their status in an organization. As you slay dragons, win accounts, overcome market obstacles, and grow a business, it is human to develop admiration for and appreciation of those with whom you serve. On the flip side, these bonds made at work are not unbreakable.

Friendships born from work have the potential to end poorly and/or dramatically. You may have built a trusting relationship only to discover your trust was violated. You may have a friend reporting to you who is failing at the job, and after attempts to correct their actions, you must terminate the work relationship. This has the potential to damage the entire relationship. And, yes, it usually does. Ending work relationships often leads to disappointment.

Some of the most disappointing conclusions to relationships for me have come from work relationships that needed to end at work. At the same time, there was no willingness or maturity to continue the relationships once the individuals were no longer employed.

John D. Rockefeller once said, "A friendship founded on business is better than a business founded on friendship."[27] I've seen this play out to be true. In the cooperative pursuit of building an organization or defeating a competitor comes comradery. You are all in the foxhole together. There are company celebrations for milestones and successes. There

---

27   "John D. Rockefeller Quotes," BrainyQuote.com, accessed July 16, 2023, https://www.brainyquote.com/quotes/john_d_rockefeller_103600.

are strategy sessions, group projects, and conventions. There are trips together, which build connections and experiences. You can choose not to build close relationships through these interactions, but then the disingenuousness of such actions will keep trust from building and demotivate virtuous people, defeating the purpose.

I was taught early in my career not to develop friendships at work. I was told to keep a firm separation so I could act without emotion when making personnel changes. I kept a wall up around my personal life. I did this because I was told it would keep people from using my experiences to manipulate me. I was taught to see people as a resource that could be used when needed and eliminated when not. This would put friendship at work squarely within Aristotle's friendships of utility.

With time, I learned this is not possible if you want to encourage and develop teams. It is better to be genuine and open yourself up to being disappointed by a relationship rather than to shut people out. Twice I changed jobs in my career because the leaders I was serving kept me at arm's length and were unwilling to open their world fully to me for learning and comradery. I had no interest in taking on the world *for* someone, but I was more than willing to slay dragons *with* someone. Let me tell you a story about this. . . .

In 1995, I met a gentleman who owned an insurance agency in the Dallas Fort Worth (DFW) metroplex. His name was Al Boenker. He had built a business and a highly recognized brand in DFW. He was a client of the company I was working for in the media world, and I was given the responsibility of managing his account. The more time I spent with him, the more I was impressed with his style of leadership. He was the sort of individual who was willing to teach, listen, and include me in the things he was doing. He taught me business lessons with each of our interactions, as he was twenty years my senior.

In 1998 I went to work for Al Boenker. He permitted me access to all departments within his business, not just the one I was managing. He encouraged learning and licensing, and he included me in the new ventures he took on and the companies he built. He never spoke down to me. He permitted me to make mistakes. He offered counsel. He also included me in the personal parts of his life, his family, and his personal trips. He followed a completely different pattern than the individuals I had served in the past. He opened the door and gave me access to his business and his life.

Twenty-five years later, I am grateful for a long career within one organization, but more grateful for being treated as a friend and not an employee. This was not unique to me. Al did the same for everyone on his leadership team and others who had spent many years with the company. Al never kept people at arm's length —he brought them in with a bear hug.

Al's example broke the mold I had been poured into during my media career. His process was not cutthroat but inclusive. It was a virtuous example of a path to success. There are many ways to succeed, but a virtuous path provides a great deal more satisfaction when the goal is achieved and you find you are not standing alone on the podium.

Al's example reflects the process of treating everyone with sincerity and the hope that a relationship can move into a primary friendship. As a leader, you can be a mentor and share with employees your past lessons learned. You can also learn lessons together in the battle to build a company. This give-and-take creates an unbreakable bond.

If you are the employee and are given such an opportunity, there are some important steps you must take to make this relationship work well and to ensure you take a virtuous approach. First, you can be grateful for being treated as a friend, but you must never stop behaving as an employee. Obligations and duties must be met, but most importantly, respect must be given without acting in an overly familiar tone. You must continue to permit yourself to be invited and never intrude. You should never assume or behave as if the friendship releases you from responsibilities or elevates you over others in the organization. You mustn't be jealous when others are given the same access. Finally, you must never use your relationship with a supervisor to coerce or frighten others. When people in leadership give you access to their lives, you are given a great responsibility.

Relationships with leaders in a company require you to ensure you are keeping your actions virtuous and to step carefully with the kindness you've been shown. Leaders may step down from their platforms, but you cannot step up to theirs without an invitation.

A parable told by Jesus is the best example for an employee on how to behave when invited into a friendship by someone in leadership. The Gospel of Luke recalls Jesus saying,

> "When someone invites you to a wedding feast, do not take the place of honor, for a person more distinguished than you may have been invited. If so, the host who invited both of you will come and say to you, 'Give this person your seat.' Then, humiliated, you will have to take the least important place. But when you are invited, take the lowest place, so that when your host comes, he will say to you, 'Friend, move up to a better place.' Then you will be honored in the presence of all the other guests. For all those who exalt themselves will be humbled, and those who humble themselves will be exalted." (Luke 14:8–11)

Jesus encourages us to serve and not to assume an air of authority or elevated position. He says to let the true authority—be it your manager, company ownership, or another—decide how things should proceed.

By submitting to authority, as in serving a friend, we avoid harming the relationship. Our actions may put our leaders at rest, in that they are not concerned about us taking authority from them or making them look as if they are not in control.

By serving and submitting, we give them room to bless us with growth in our roles, pay, and influence.

How much more do we enjoy the fruits of our efforts when they are recognized by those we serve and awarded to us? This is much sweeter than taking what we think we deserve and, in the process, potentially creating discord.

Here is another example: I had a test for new hires on our executive team. I would invite some of the leadership team out to lunch. If the new person jumped in the front seat without offering it to someone else, I immediately made a judgment on his or her future within our organization. Never take the seat of honor, and always elevate those you serve above yourself.

If you are a leader, you can choose how to serve others. I've followed Al's pattern and opened my personal life to those around me, knowing there are potential perils in such actions but willing to be disappointed over being disconnected.

In my work relationships I have built lifelong brothers and sisters, and I have also built lifelong enemies. Understand that when one of these relationships goes in a poor direction and you must make a business decision to separate, there is a high probability the other person will not forgive you for that decision. Poor performance, bad behavior, apathy, unkindness, and other negatives cannot be tolerated in an organization. Such things can rot the performance of a company. No matter how close you may be to someone, you may eventually have to make the tough call of termination—as well as deal with other types of conflict.

I want to discuss conflict in friendship in more detail in a later chapter, but let me state here that as it relates to friendships within the framework of business, we must be willing to engage in debate with one another and hold varying opinions about business matters. Debate must be done with respect, with supporting data, and with passionate conviction. We must be willing to lose the debate. If we do win it, we need to show grace to the other party. In business there are countless unknowns, and we cannot be certain if our decision is going to be the winner or loser for an organization. The goal is to achieve success together, which means we need all minds and ideas in the arena.

Aristotle spoke of the friendships of utility and pleasure. These were seen as temporal. In life, and within business, we must not use others for our gain or, worse, dismiss the relationship when goals are reached. Including people and journeying together keep us from using others. Further, and especially in business, we cannot take advantage of others for pleasure or for our amusement. Relationships must be built from respect and the journey enjoyed together.

Elevate those working hard around you. Respect and promote them, and always put them before yourself. Be open, kind, and inclusive. Give all the successes to them, and reserve all the blame for yourself. At the same time, do not be afraid of conflict, correction, or terminating those who could negatively impact your business or team. Be willing to deal with the great discomfort that comes with these decisions as you guard those you serve.

There is no doubt about it. Terminating someone is a horrible experience. Terminating someone or ending a work relationship with someone you have built a friendship with is excruciating. I've seldom been forgiven after a termination or separation. Remember, primary friendship is built between virtuous people. If someone is failing in service, treating others in the company poorly, behaving in a deceitful manner, or not taking steps to correct noted items, then this is not a person for your inner circle.

Some of the folks from my inner circle began from friendships at work. Most of them are men, and this booklet is generally about friendships between men, but I want to address friendship in the workplace between those of the opposite sex. If you want to create an open environment that provides opportunities for everyone, you'll need to be inclusive in your work relationships. If you exclude women (or members of the opposite sex) from friendship in the office, you'll create a "good ol' boy" network. This can prevent women in the workplace from equal opportunity and growth. If you live out a pattern of true friendship, you can develop great relationships with your work companions, both male and female. There are dangers in close relationships between people of the opposite sex; however, two virtuous people can work well together and enjoy a great friendship. Let's look at one of my personal examples.

I have worked with Maria Cortez for twenty years. I've watched her grow in our company and create and manage processes and programs that have generated millions in profit for our organization. I travel with her over eight weeks a year, setting up companies in foreign countries. I have spent weekends on business trips hanging out by the pool with her. I admire her commitment, successes, leadership, and family life, and I enjoy her company. She is a dear friend—a true friend.

For a decade, small people have gossiped about us and spread stories that were untrue and hurtful. Other women even participated, making a woman look small by spreading lies and ultimately promoting the practice of exclusion by generating such gossip. Maria is a C-suite individual who has earned her success, and there is no reason for my fellow worker and sister not to be included in my inner circle.

I have learned important lessons from my relationship with her. For one, our working relationships should not be exclusively based on gender. Basing them on gender would ultimately make our inner circle less inclusive and wouldn't allow expansion of the opportunities for those we serve with daily. Service and trust are the keys, which brings up another issue.

If your spouse does not trust you because you have proven yourself unworthy of managing relationships with others, then you have no business in leading a business. If your wife does not trust you because of her insecurities, then you have something to work on as a couple. The standards of virtue should be promoted within the goals of all organizations.

I want to restate this. There are many ways to success, but the virtuous path, the open path—the inclusive path—offer the greatest satisfaction when success does arrive. Plus, these paths open the possibility of creating lifelong primary friendships. After all, success not shared is a vain pursuit.

Chapter 10

A VISIT FROM ATHENA

*T*HE *ODYSSEY* IS ONE OF THE GREATEST ADVENTURE STORIES OF ALL TIME. From it, we receive the term "mentor," offering Telemachus's story as an example.

Telemachus's father, Odysseus, had been fighting in the battle of Troy and for some time delayed returning home to his family. Odysseus was believed by the nobles of Ithaca to be dead; consequently, his wife had many suitors at their island home. Telemachus was in great danger as the son of Odysseus because the suiters would not stand for the potential of the next generation revolting against them. The goddess Athena was well engaged with Odysseus and helped him throughout his journey home. She also appeared to Telemachus as a man named Mentor. Mentor encouraged Telemachus to rise up against his mother's suiters and seek the whereabouts of his father. As the epic progresses, we see Telemachus grow into a responsible man. He may not have done so without the mentorship of Mentor.

One of the most important types of relationships is a mentor-mentee relationship, which is foundational to building wisdom and kinship and moving society in the right direction. However, this type of relationship is fading away in the fabric of modern society.

Strangely, we now have adults looking to emulate young people—not young people wanting to grow up to be like the elders in their lives. I saw this change as my kids were entering middle school and high school, and it confused me. They are so different from me when I was growing up. For example, when I was in church youth groups, the youth pastors wore suits on Sunday to church services and were building their careers in ministry, aiming to be lead church pastors. These men were kind and engaging with young people, but they were also careful not to be too familiar. We thought it amazing they would let us call them by their first names, but that was as familiar as we were permitted to be.

At any rate, when my kids started youth group, I really noticed the differences. The men leading youth groups wore flip-flops and t-shirts. They listened to the same music as the kids and let the youth call them names like "Steve-O" and "Bigs." It was as if their exposure to young people hindered these men from being great at interacting with men their own age, as if they had forgotten how.

Case in point, let me tell you about the talk I had with my son. He was headed off to church camp one summer, and I had a short conversation with him before he left. "Son, church camp is fun, and it's also a time to learn and experience God in a relaxed setting. The people leading will at some point ask if God is calling you into full-time ministry. The answer to that is of course, he *is* calling you into full-time ministry—that is what life is about. But these men will be referring to the way they minister. Working at a church full time. Chances are very slim this is what God is calling you to. But know this—men who stand up in front of you dressed sloppily, who have silly beards and don't take care of themselves, are not something you want to be when you grow up. You want to dress like an adult, talk like an adult, and behave in a manner that shows your maturity and wisdom. Don't fall for, or into, their immaturity."

When I asked him how camp went upon his return, he stated, "It went just like you said it would." Case closed.

Here is the bottom line: Virtuous friends are people who are investing in their own growth. In turn, they invest in yours. They are lifelong learners and committed to changing when they encounter the truth. Often a younger generation has something to teach the world, but seldom does a young person have a lesson to teach an older one. However, this does not mean we should be dismissive of young people or not listen to them. As an older generation, we must know the questions of the next generation and be prepared to answer them in a way they understand. This is where the mentor-mentee relationship comes in.

Relationships between generations, and even between contemporaries, offer an opportunity to grow friendships into the mentor-mentee category. A young person with a desire to gain wisdom from someone older and an older person willing to take the time to listen as well as teach can change societies. Let me take a moment to explain by showing some examples of mentors from my life. . . .

I've shared about Don Staton and David Bertch and their profound impact on my life. There is a long list of older gentlemen and women who took the time to be a part of my life and, in doing so, imparted wisdom that would be hard to find without their time, example, and words. For example, Steve French was my youth pastor during my most formative years. He set a great example of a young husband and leader. He was a deep and thoughtful teacher. He was a listener and an encourager. He did not accept immature behavior and offered correction. He gave trust and the opportunity to fail. His influence impacted my entire younger life, and later when I was in my fifties, he continued to influence me when I asked him to spend six months meeting with me on a non-profit project I was working on. He continues to spend his life mentoring others.

When my family moved to Texas, a youth leader named Robert Garrett reflected Steve's approach. He was kind and available but kept proper boundaries and set a mature example.

Robert was engaging and available to youth while also providing an adult image. He carried himself as a professional and was building a family. He made time for them instead of creating an endless amount of youth programs he would have to attend and manage. Both he and his wife provided an example of a healthy marriage.

Scott and Hylda Williams taught college-aged students on Sundays at our church when I was dating Danae. They offered relationship counseling and encouraged us in countless ways. Scott offered me a summer job where I learned career lessons from him about hard work and commitment. He is the grandfather of our daughter-in-law and is still setting an example for Danae and me thirty-five years later.

My boss, Al Boenker, has been a mentor to me. He has taught me endless career lessons in business management and how to manage surprises and difficulties, but he has also taught me how to hunt and work a farm. He invited me to worm goats and plow fields, introducing a greenhorn like me to new things.

My close contemporaries who are ten years older than I am, Richard Sammons and Britt Lane, have taught me many life lessons. Richard invited me on my first trip to Europe and introduced me to the friends and places he loved throughout Germany. He taught me how to appreciate wine and how to pair it with a meal. Britt owned his own business and would give impromptu lessons on managing government agencies and keeping up with compliance. He helped me understand the legal landscapes and best practices.

My father was also a mentor. He gave me access to new places and experiences and coached me through dinners with colleagues. He taught me about table manners in nice restaurants. And what I am most grateful for is his giving me a love for the outdoors in the many places he and my mom took my brother and me.

My mother was a mentor dedicated to teaching. She spent every evening in the hallway with my brother and me, sharing stories from the Bible and praying with and for us.

Her greatest concern was our coming to faith in Jesus. She provided not only the input for our minds, but the prayer for our souls.

I met Clint May when we were attending Wedgwood Baptist Church in Fort Worth, Texas. He managed the children's ministry. Clint believed children had the ability to teach the gospel and lead other young people into a life of faith. He would teach them how to interact with other kids, ask questions, and take an interest in their lives. He would then have the kids he trained run entire summer camps for other young people with some adult oversight. The children he taught, including our children, gained incredible life skills and wisdom as early as age nine. The maturity of the kids was profound, and many have continued to invest in others with the lessons learned from Clint and his "Leaders in Training" program.

A mentor can be any age. If you are a teenager, you can help a middle schooler improve at a sport, feel loved and welcomed, and assist him in moving through the waters of adolescence. It's never too early to begin your life as a mentor. I use David Bertch's example. When I perceive a young person wants to grow, I invite him to read a book with me and meet to discuss the book. This has opened countless friendships where I am permitted to impart wisdom from lessons and experiences in my life. As I meet with young men, I learn also. I learn the questions and needs of their generation. I learn the way they use language, and I learn what lessons and advice might best serve them.

In our casual and business interactions, we must be open to being a mentor to someone and quick to identify how we may serve them. This may be for daily living, business, sports, hobbies, or other interests. If we have experiences and knowledge that interest them, or might interest them, we need to open ourselves up for interaction. To be a mentor is to live up to life's great responsibility of engaging across generational lines and imparting wisdom through a permission-based, virtuous friendship. To elevate another person with such high regard, you want to ensure you share with them the most important lessons you've learned in life. Friendships built like this last a lifetime.

We must also be open to building friendships as the mentee. There is much to learn from so many interesting and different people. The simple task of asking someone to invest in you will in most cases open the door to lifelong friendship. Most people want to share their experiences and knowledge, but it is hard for them to find an interested listener.

In building friendships, we must intentionally seek and recognize where we may serve in the mentor role—not out of our desire to talk or be heard but from a desire to be available and to listen. The action of listening and caring will give us permission to share wisdom. Athena transformed into Mentor, and we too can transform into this role to care for those around us.

Look for those around you who have good relationships and have lived life well, experienced successes, and overcome adversity. Then ask them if they would be willing to invest in you. What a joy it will be for them, and what a benefit it will be for you.

Chapter 11

THE TWO-YEAR RELATIONSHIP

Ernest Hemingway is famously attributed with saying, "The best way to find out if you can trust somebody is to trust them."[28] It is this simple. You, as an individual who has chosen to live virtuously, must decide to place your trust in someone, knowing there is always a possibility of being disappointed. If your trust is violated, then you must determine if the relationship is repairable.

It will take two years before you can know if you have a true friendship with another person. Time and experience are the only ways to measure trust. You must have experiences that include conflict—the way you move through conflict is the greatest identifier of a virtuous friendship.

The truth is, everyone will disappoint you at some point—some in minor ways and others with major violations of your trust. You will also disappoint others, even if that is not your

---

28   Ernest Hemingway, "Ernest Hemingway Quotes," BrainyQuote.com, accessed July 20, 2023, https://www.brainyquote.com/quotes/ernest_hemingway_383691.

intention. Often your words or actions will be misunderstood, taken the wrong way, or simply ignored. At any rate, if you get to know someone well enough, you will undergo this conflict phase, along with many other challenges.

You are probably familiar with the term "honeymoon phase." Upon meeting someone, you may find them witty, entertaining, insightful, and pleasant to be around. That is the honeymoon phase of the relationship. However, through time and interaction, you learn what is under the surface and decide whether there is value in placing time and effort into the relationship. You may also meet someone you perceive has potential but is lacking in wisdom or experience. When that happens, you must decide whether to invest yourself in the individual in order to create opportunities for them. There is no way to know how the relationship will go. Only time will tell. Eventually, you'll have a disagreement, a debate, or an action one of you finds questionable—this conflict will be the true test of where the relationship will go.

I have a saying for my friends: "If I didn't love you, I would not share with you the most important convictions in my life. It is because I love you, I passionately share my convictions."

Disagreement with another's convictions can be good for relationships. Friends who challenge each other will have conflict but can find ways to move through it and come out the other side with a potentially deeper friendship. Ways to live, politics, religion, faith, education, science, finances, philosophy, relationships, and other topics should be on the table of discussion at all times between friends. These are the ideas that form us and build our thoughts, and friends should help each other formulate their thoughts and positions.

The time we have on planet earth is short, so we should engage in discussion and debate about ideas we are passionate about. I've discovered some of my most valued friendships are with virtuous men who think differently than I do. I may at times even consider some of their ideas unvirtuous, but I understand their convictions about these ideas and permit them to attempt to persuade me. I have friends who are atheists, liberals, far right, pro-choice, Trumpers, climate-change deniers, and a long list of positions I may or may not hold, but I still listen to them in our discussions and consider why they formulate their ideas as they do.

What a shame we now live in a society where people who disagree hate each other. Or if differences are discovered, relationships end. Someone who will end a friendship over a political discussion lacks virtue. In friendship, we care so much for our "second self," we continue to find ways to influence with kindness and commitment.

Cicero wrote this in his *Treatises*:

> It often happens that friends need remonstrance and reproof. When these are administered in a kindly spirit they ought to be taken on good part ... but the man ... is most to blame if he resents plain speaking and allows flattery to egg him on to his ruin. On this point then from first to last

there is need of deliberation and care. If we remonstrate, it should be without bitterness: if we reprove there should be no word of insult.[29]

Friendship should be based on what is true. If we identify a concern in a friend's behavior or action, we are being a good friend when we address it with them in kindness and concern. It's possible they may be making decisions from emotion or with a lack of thought.

My faith is the driving force behind my decision making. If all the people around me feel the same as I do, who is there to persuade? If my faith is the most important force in my life and I don't share it, aren't I behaving as if it had no value? If I do not share my convictions with those who feel differently, aren't I behaving disrespectfully toward them?

Some may shy away from disagreement out of a sense of respect for their friends, but we should be open to conflict in our friendships. We must trust the other person is sharing, reproofing, correcting, or discussing topics out of concern for us. The battle of ideas should be a treasure in friendship as we share our convictions out of love for the other person. After the conflict, however, we must also be open to agreeing to disagree and realign with all we do have in common, remembering our care for the other person. Let me share a story with you. . . .

My friend Trevor Sabsook was going through a difficult time about fifteen years ago. He felt as if he were at rock bottom.

29   Cicero, *Treatises on Friendship and Old Age*, trans. E. S. Shuckburgh (New York: Another Leaf Press, 2009), 39.

Part of the Christian faith is to share our faith with others and offer them the opportunity to put their faith in Christ. As a result, I told Trevor I wanted to share something with him that was very important to me about faith in Jesus Christ and how my faith had pulled me through very difficult times. At the end of our discussion, I offered him the opportunity to put his faith in Jesus.

Trevor told me it wasn't for him. He just did not see things the way I did, and he did not want to make a decision about Jesus.

I told him I understood.

His next question was, "What happens now?" I was confused by the question and stated I didn't know what he meant. He told me other people had shared their faith in Jesus with him, and when he didn't agree with them, they discontinued the friendship. For me, this was a heartbreaking statement. How could people who shared the same faith as I make a demand instead of an offer? If getting immediate agreement was the only choice, how would Christians ever build true friendships with others?

I told Trevor I was his friend no matter the choices he did or did not make about faith in his life. Since that day we've had other conversations about faith, and we still do not agree. Trevor is a committed and caring friend, and I want what is best for him. He wants the same for me. We disagree on an important topic in my life, but we have plenty in common, care for one another, and have the ability to move through conflict.

Our ability to engage in the battle of ideas and permit conflict is what makes our relationship wonderful.

On the other hand, conflict related to poor actions may be different. Lies, half-truths, fraud, and other violations must be thoroughly considered before moving forward in a relationship. One party or both must confess their failures and establish a desire not to repeat them. One or both parties must be open to forgiveness and a willingness to move past the offense.

Some violations of trust may be forgiven but make it impossible to reengage in the friendship once known. Cicero writes this:

> It will happen at times that an outbreak of vicious conduct affects either a man's friends themselves or strangers, yet the discredit falls on the friends. In such cases friendships should be allowed to die out gradually by an intermission of intercourse . . . unless, indeed, the injurious conduct be of so violent and outrageous a nature to make an instant breach and separation the only possible course consistent with honor and rectitude. [30]

Some actions and events may be forgiven, but the impact may make it difficult to continue to pursue an affectionate relationship. Cicero recommends a quiet exit from the relationship over time instead of an instant proclamation to never see one another again.

---

[30] Cicero, introductory note in *Treatises*.

Dramatic separations create long-term pain. Cutting someone off from communication, excluding them from a group or family, or engaging in a screaming match with no resolve are examples. You may end up harboring resentment instead of offering forgiveness in such separations. While you may not be given a choice, if possible, move away from caustic or difficult friendships quietly to avoid creating outright public discord.

I've experienced vicious conflicts with a few friends in my fifty-three years. While I hold to my convictions and the rightness of my anger, I confess a failure in my process of separation. I could have gone away quietly, created less drama, and maybe saved some hope of reconciliation later; however, I did not take Cicero's advice and allowed friendships to die out through a lack of interaction. I did see the behavior of these individuals as harmful to others, but it was a battle of ideas, not physical harm, and I should have walked away quietly, for Cicero continues . . .

> For there can be nothing more discreditable than to be at open war with a man with whom you have been intimate . . . our friendship should seem to have died a natural rather than a violent death.[31]

I've learned to take Cicero's advice in the past decade by stepping away quietly when facing an unresolvable conflict.

---

31   Cicero, *Treatises*, 35.

No proclamations of disagreeability need be made. Usually, the person you are having conflict with will change the pattern of communication to less frequent interaction. There is also no need to be unkind at any time.

As I have stated, separations should be the great exception to conflict. It should be possible to resolve most disagreements or disappointing actions between virtuous people. My Christian faith says all people are sinners, and all people fail. If God offers us grace, we must also offer grace to others.

You will likely get the opportunity to offer grace after you've known someone for a couple of years. As I've mentioned, I've found that's when conflict will generally come— within the first two years of a relationship. Two years gives time for the personality of a person to completely reveal itself. This is true with all relationships, even at work with employees, vendors, and clients. Markets change and contracts must be renegotiated, products and processes sometimes fail, and then comes the test of the relationship. If you move through the conflict well, you should have a friendship of greater value.

Kindness must be the controlling factor of conflict and conviction. An opposing view is never changed by hatred and separation. As we engage with our friends and potential friends, we must let kindness drive the bus. Kindness and an open mind. Offer your trust to others and be willing to be disappointed; when disappointment comes, determine how to move through your conflict with a desire to reconcile and forgive. Sure, there will be times in your life when you respond incorrectly, or violate the trust of someone else, or need reproof. But remember to be open to listening, learning, and asking for forgiveness. If you can do this, you will build deeper and more trustworthy relationships.

Chapter 12

YOUR MOST IMPORTANT FRIEND– YOUR SPOUSE

"FOR NOTHING IS GREATER OR BETTER THAN THIS, WHEN MAN AND WIFE DWELL IN A HOME IN ONE ACCORD, A GREAT GRIEF TO THEIR FOES [185] AND A JOY TO THEIR FRIENDS; BUT THEY KNOW IT BEST THEMSELVES," WROTE HOMER IN *THE ODYSSEY*.[32] Your spouse is the most important friendship of your life. Together, as a team, you can confound your enemies and delight your friends while experiencing the great institution of marriage.

There is no doubt about it: Friendship in marriage requires consistent effort. It is a relationship where the term "second self" should be in bold caps and underlined. The choice to marry and move through the entire course of your life with one other individual is a commitment to elevate your second self to a sacred position. You do not marry for what the other can do

---

32   Homer, *The Odyssey*, trans. A. T. Murray, vol. 1 (Cambridge, MA: Harvard University Press, 1919), bk. VI, line 185.

for you; you marry because your love and fidelity for your wife is so great you want above all in life to improve her life.

Marriage is a powerful, world-changing institution. Without it, we are not just losing ground in serving our society and another person, but we are also losing foundational friendships. Consider the following statistics:

> Since the start of the 21st century, the U.S. marriage rate has declined from more than eight marriages per 1,000 down to six marriages per 1,000 population in 2019. That marriage rate is the lowest level since the U.S. government began keeping marriage records for the country in 1867. Also, 70 years ago a large majority of U.S. households, approximately 80 percent, were made up of married couples. In 2020, the proportion of households consisting of married couples fell to 49 percent.[33]

An institution foundational to productive societies is declining at an alarming rate within two generations. But why are young people choosing not to get married?

Clarissa Sawyer, lecturer in natural and applied sciences, cites reasons for this decline in marriage among millennials as highlighted in a Bentley University article, "Why Millennials Refuse to Get Married" by Kristen Walsh. People are waiting to get married for numerous reasons in our modern society. According to Sawyer, fear of divorce is a leading reason. She

---

33   Joseph Chamie, "The end of marriage in America?," The Hill, August 8, 2021, https://thehill.com/opinion/finance/567107-the-end-of-marriage-in-america/.

points out, "Millennials . . . take time to get to know their partner, accumulate assets and become financially successful."[34]

Economics playing a role in fewer people getting married is not new. Economics delayed marriages during the Great Depression as jobs were scarce, and there was a fear of not being able to provide. The coming-of-age generation, however, has taken this further with their need to feel "successful" before getting married. This is a different target for everyone and is hard to define.

One of the biggest concerns I've seen in young people is a fear of getting their hearts broken. As we have discussed, we must trust to build friendship, and there is always the possibility another human will exhibit untrustworthy behavior.

Consequently, marriage makes us incredibly vulnerable to being hurt in a grand way. I've seen friends crushed under the weight of a spouse's infidelity. Some recovered and trusted someone in a new relationship. Others forgave and continued their relationship. Still others divorced and are caught in a cycle of poor decisions or even depression.

C. S. Lewis wrote this in his book *The Four Loves*:

> To love at all is to be vulnerable. Love anything and your heart will be wrung and possibly broken. If you want to make sure of keeping it intact you must give it to no one, not

---

34   Kristen Walsh, "NowUKnow: Why Millennials Refuse to Get Married," Newsroom, Bentley University, October 7, 2021, https://www.bentley.edu/news/nowuknow-why-millennials-refuse-get-married.

even an animal. Wrap it carefully round with hobbies and little luxuries; avoid all entanglements. Lock it up safe in the casket or coffin of your selfishness. But in that casket, safe, dark, motionless, airless, it will change. It will not be broken; it will become unbreakable, impenetrable, irredeemable. To love is to be vulnerable.[35]

Vulnerability does not mean foolishly or blindly running into a relationship. Vulnerability is ensuring you are honest and communicative and a listener. It means you are willing to take responsibility in a growing relationship to know and care for someone and willing to move through the difficulties of learning about another's personality and preferences. Vulnerability is trusting.

It takes a while to be truly vulnerable with someone. The two-year friendship is a viable model to get to know someone and to work through conflict as you consider a lifelong commitment to your most important friendship. This is not a foolproof method, however. Those who have known each other for weeks and months have lived long, happy friendships together just as those who dated for years. Danae and I dated for six years before getting married and still had much to work on in our relationship after we were wed. A lifelong commitment to a second self brings a lifetime of various challenges and conflicts to manage.

---

35   C. S. Lewis, *The Four Loves* (New York: Harcourt Brace Jovanovich Publishers, 1960), 169.

Life can challenge this friendship unlike any other. For example, you may commit to a person who develops medical issues later in life. Marriage may put you in a situation where you must manage a relationship with someone who has mental health issues. Your wife may lose her ability to control her body, requiring special care from you. You might have to help her through a long legal battle. She may become physically unappealing to you because of weight or age. If you chose this person because of her virtue and saw her at one time as a second self, you as a virtuous individual must live out your commitment to serve her and work through countless changes over time and the endless number of difficulties life may present. This is the purpose of the institution of marriage—to display the virtuosity of friendship to the world.

Seneca, in the known portions of his *De Matrimonio*, alludes to marriage as a state of stability that leads to virtue. The commitment through hardship is the virtuous example. The conflicts that might end marriage should be very few and should be linked to actions of extreme lack of virtue.

As a Christian, I subscribe to only one viable reason to end your lifelong commitment to your greatest friend—infidelity. Every couple I know who has decided to work through infidelity and stay together has ended in divorce later or lived a life of misery. I understand there are purposes in suffering and lessons to be gained from it, but if the God of the universe says it's a cause for separation, I think we should heed his option. Consider the following scripture: "And I say to you, whoever divorces his wife, except for sexual immorality, and marries another, commits adultery; and whoever marries her who is divorced commits adultery" (Matthew 19:9 NKJV).

From a non-biblical view, if someone is in an abusive relationship in the form of physical harm or extreme mental abuse, standing on the words of the ancients, I say this is a relationship to be ended. This should also be considered if children in the family are subjected to physical abuse or extreme mental abuse. I use the term "extreme" only as it relates to mental abuse. Any type of mental abuse should be taken seriously and professional help sought to determine what might be taking place and what should be addressed and how. If the abuse is physical—*run* for help.

I fear someone may exaggerate mental abuse and extend it to the statement "I'm not happy" or "They don't make me happy." Happiness is a fleeting feeling that comes and goes. It has been elevated by current generations to the most important goal in life. This is dangerous. Telling someone to "do what makes you happy" is as dangerous as advising them to jog on the 405 in Los Angeles. We should encourage people to "do what is virtuous" or "do what helps others."

The younger generations were raised mostly under a broad religious humanism. The self is in charge and gets to make its own rules, whether they fit into reality or not, whether established or under review, whether ancient or new, whether tested by centuries or by minutes.

Author John Zmirak of *Disorientation: How to Go to College Without Losing Your Mind* writes,

> Our country has gradually shifted from an intolerant (ca. 1688) to a tolerant (ca. 1783) Protestant culture, to a broadly religious humanism (ca. 1945), to embrace after 1968 a new and crasser creed. The lowest common denominator on which we can all agree boils down to this: suffering is worse than being happy and being alive is better than being dead—except if it means that you will suffer. That is the sum total of what Americans can agree on, the fighting creed of the free world for which we expect our soldiers to march off and die. The triumph of this new religion is everywhere apparent. . . . The God of the Happy Moments is a jealous god, and his zealots are proving to be bigots.[36]

If happiness is the goal of our lives, we are in serious trouble, as this fickle feeling is always fleeting. The moment we think we are happy, the events of life will take the happiness from us.

The ancients had a much different view of happiness than moderns. For Aristotle, happiness is an "activity of the soul that expresses virtue."[37] According to him, all things in the universe have purpose. His famous example is the acorn's purpose of becoming a thriving oak. For Aristotle, humankind is the only creature given the power of reason, and this gift is to be used

---

36   John Zmirak, "The Devil in Harvard Yard," May 14, 2014, ISI Archive, Intercollegiate Studies Institute, https://isi.org/intercollegiate-review/the-devil-in-harvard-yard/.

37   Aristotle, *Nicomachean Ethics*, trans. Joe Sachs (London: Penguin Classics, 2003), bk. II, ch. 6, lines 1106b22–23.

to make decisions to live virtuously. Happiness is not a fleeting feeling but a way of living.

The ancient biblical view of happiness is related to a way of living and the condition of the heart. These ancient paths are not focused on the self in whole, but mostly on our call to responding virtuously to the elements and events surrounding us. It is the aim to produce love, joy, peace, patience, kindness, goodness, and self-control. Again, the aim is virtue. The point is this: Friendship in marriage thrives under these definitions and applications of happiness. This form of friendship, marriage, requires us to carefully consider whom we are willing to serve our entire life.

How do you live out your greatest friendship? Your wife must be the friend you place before all others. Most of your time and energy are to be focused on her. You sacrifice your wants and needs if necessary to serve her and help her achieve her goals. Virtue would have both friends behaving the same, creating an atmosphere of support, compromise, and equality that helps each individual grow and progress. This comes through time together and constant and open communication. This friendship requires forgiveness and leaving failures in the past. The lessons learned in marriage in serving each other may be applied to all friendships. Marriage is sealed with vows as a covenant relationship, and you can apply this same attitude to other friendships in your life.

There is something incredibly unique, however, about friendship within marriage that should never be shared with others: sexual intimacy, which should be considered sacrosanct. Sex in marriage should be frequent, fun, and passionate. It is the one thing you share that no one else knows or understands about the two of you, a place where no one else will ever be in your relationship. Sex is affirming, comforting, and euphoric. It binds two individuals in a mystical way.

The modern culture has made the mistake of making sex about one's own personal pleasure, moving it to a place of recreation instead of a special gift between two committed lifelong friends. Marriages suffer when one or both individuals bring their sexual experiences with others to the marriage, which may lead to comparison and disappointment. If one or both had sex with others before marriage, this should be addressed in detail before committing to marriage, for awareness and understanding of each other's life journey and the potential difficulties it could bring. Furthermore, even without considering a biblical view of sex and marriage at all, it is still evident sex in marriage is a much more enjoyable and satisfying act that binds two people in a unique way when they have never shared the act with anyone outside of the relationship.

There is also a level of emotional intimacy to be shared between you and your wife. Emotional intimacy is a part of all friendships at some level, but between you and your spouse at a much deeper level. This may include secrets, shared fears, and failures, and both partners should define what they wish not to be shared with others.

Experiences should be sought in your friendship with your spouse as you seek shared interests and adventures. Life together should be creating stories that will become a quilt of memories as you grow older. This looks very different for various personalities, but the process of discovery is a wonderful journey.

Having offspring is part of this journey. It is virtuous to have children and to parent them together. This is one of the great shared adventures of life and one of the gifts that drains us of our selfishness and prepares us in our service to others.

For example, children require massive amounts of time and investment. Since they are our offspring, we are prone to live up to our obligations to them. The care of children demands we give up on our selfishness by putting their interests over ours, giving up time reserved for ourselves in the past, and putting extra effort into our work to ensure we are able to provide. These actions will diminish our selfishness.

If other friendships are complicated, then marriage is even more so. The consideration of marrying someone should come with deep reflection and investigation. The commitment of marriage should be considered sacred and lifelong. The process of marriage should be selfless, with a deep focus on the other person's care and growth. There should be no other friendship in your life on the same level.

The wonderful gift of working on our marriage is learning the skills needed to serve well and to become a better friend to others in our life. This is done by virtue.

If we live out friendship in marriage in a virtuous way, we will build strong families, strong communities, and strong cultures. The institution of marriage is the most sacred of friendships and refines us and prepares us to serve all as we serve the one person we care about most in life.

Chapter 13

THE CASE FOR FRIENDSHIP

I F YOU HAPPENED TO READ THE POEM IN THE FRONT MATTER
OF THIS BOOK, I'D LIKE TO POINT OUT THAT IT WAS ONE OF
MANY POEMS WRITTEN BY GAIUS VALERIUS CATULLUS, 84–54
BC. Catullus was a contemporary and friend of Cicero. Like
Valerius, I'd like for you to "keep for your own this little book
such as it is, and whatever it is worth; and may it, O Virgin my
patroness, live and last for more than one century."[38] I hope my
words have influenced you in the way of friendship, but let us
turn again to Catullus, who wrote of his friend Cicero:

> Most skilled in speech of the descendants of Romulus, all
> who are, all who have been, and all who shall be hereafter
> in other years Marcus Tullius—to thee his warmest thanks
> Catullus gives, the worst of all poets, as much as the worst
> poet of all as you are the best advocate of all.[39]

38   Catullus, *The Poems of Gaius Valerius Catullus*, (Cambridge, MA: Harvard
University Press, 1962; reprinted with corrections, 2017), 3.
39   Cicero, Poem XLIX in *Treatises on Friendship and Old Age*, trans. by E. S.
Shuckburgh (New York: Another Leaf Press, 2009), 57.

In his lines, Catullus speaks of friends, lovers, and enemies at times in terms direct and even lewd for moderns. But he sings the praises of his friends. We do not often sing the praises of our friends, for we as moderns have failed to grasp the wonder and depth of the gift of true friendship. Furthermore, I hope to join countless others before, all who have said it better, and make a case for your passionate pursuit of serving others in the spirit of friendship described in my little booklet.

As you are fully aware at this point, I come with the presupposition that the God of the Bible is the creator of the universe. I did not arrive at this just because my parents told me so, but I spent years seeking, searching, and studying all known options for the origin and purpose of life. I found only the person of Jesus puts all of life into order and understanding. If you disagree with me on this, you can agree with me that Jesus was himself an ancient and a teacher whose words were recorded for us to consider.

The Christian God is single-minded but multi-person. The Father, Son, and Holy Spirit are in a relationship with one another: a friendship. The Father serves the Son; the Son serves the Father; the Spirit serves the Son. Jesus as a man communicates with his Father. We have record of him going off to spend time with his Father in prayer. On one of his last days on earth, he cries out to his Father. The Spirit follows Christ's departure to be his representative to man, on his behalf communicating his teachings with humankind. The Christian God is a relational being, virtuous and serving one another.

We have relationships because God is in a relationship. Because he knows the value, beauty, and power of persons in relationships. He loves unity amongst diverse individuals. He has given us what he enjoys most, which is to be in a relationship with others. He created us to be in a relationship with him, and he created us to be in a relationship with one another. We are powerless in our need for others because we were made to be in unity with diverse persons.

Francis Schaeffer wrote the following in his book *He Is There and He Is Not Silent*:

> Every once in a while, in my discussions someone asks me how I can believe in the Trinity. My answer is always the same. I would still be an agnostic if there was no Trinity because there would be no answers. Without the high order of personal unity and diversity as given in the Trinity, there are no answers.[40]

Schaeffer encountered truth because God himself explains the value of relationships and the purpose of relationships. Relationships are part of our reality, and so God, in relationship and the creator of relationships, explains the reality in which we live and the extreme importance of a relationship with him and with others.

Indeed, the Bible is full of stories of deeply affectionate friendships and of the pain and grief from failed friendships. It

---

40   Francis Schaeffer, *He Is There and He Is Not Silent*, in *The Complete Works of Francis Schaeffer*, vol. 1 (Westchester, IL: Crossway, 1985), 288–89.

provides examples of reconciled friendships. In its pages from over forty writers over thousands of years, we are told God calls us "friend," and we are given examples of his interaction with man as a friend. Examples are found in the way he came to Moses, stood with three rebels in a fire, and sat and cooked fish with his disciples around the campfire.

God says when we commit to a relationship with him, he calls us "friend." In the book of John, Jesus says this:

> "I no longer call you servants, because a servant does not know his master's business. Instead, I have called you friends, for everything that I learned from my Father I have made known to you. You did not choose me, but I chose you and appointed you so that you might go and bear fruit—fruit that will last—and so that whatever you ask in my name the Father will give you." (John 15:15–16)

The ancients had discovered God's design of friendship in that it was a relationship between virtuous individuals. God is always virtuous, and we are made virtuous through him. He calls us to virtue and obedience. "Come near to God and he will come near to you" (James 4:8). This is the action a friend would take with another, to come close in affection, kindness, and humble admiration.

I believe God is the case for friendship. To love others the way he loves us. To sacrifice for others and to be a refuge for them in difficulty.

At the same time, the ancient pagans found the elements of truth about friendship in their search for ideas. Cicero, Seneca, and Aristotle make the case of a life well lived when lived in harmony with others. Seneca makes the case, "For what purpose, then, do I make a man my friend? In order to have someone for whom I may die, whom I may follow into exile, against whose death I may stake my own life, and pay the pledge, too."[41]

Is this the purpose of your friendships? Are the people in close relationship with you people you would die for, follow into exile, stake your own life for, and pay pledge to? If you do not have these friendships in your life, there could be no greater purpose than to seek them out and create them. Do you even speak out about your love, your pledges, your commitments?

The shallow, purposeless, brief relationships of the twenty-first century are ripping us further apart by the week. We no longer engage in a meaningful way with those around us. We retreat behind our walls and isolate ourselves, using cold technology to state our demands and dislikes and make our displays. We don't engage in a way to learn what virtues might be in a person's heart. We don't get close enough to gain permission to speak into their lives in areas where they may have it wrong; even worse, we have no one to tell us when we've got it wrong. We ultimately fail to meet their needs and serve them simply because of their humanity. We are so damnably busy worrying

---

41   Seneca, "On Benefits" (*De Beneficiis*), in *Seneca: Selected Philosophical Works*, ed. Brad Inwood and Lloyd P. Gerson (Indianapolis: Hackett Publishing Company, 2010), bk. III, section 16.

about our wants, needs, opinions, and being right, we have little awareness or want for others. Or we have filled the schedule so we don't have time to invest in others, to sit and listen with intent, to experience life with several close friends.

Even worse, we busy ourselves with relationships that entertain us or gain us access or opportunity with little concern for the welfare or wellbeing of the other. We have an endless list of work relationships with no depth and little chance of being extended past the life of the job. Worse still, we stay in so-called friendships with individuals who bring us down, drain our energy, and keep us from virtuousness.

Even worse still, we turn to ourselves in this identity culture also referred to as the "Me Culture." We push our identity as a brand and demand to be permitted to express ourselves in any form possible, whether under any virtuous banner or not, as we somehow feel it is important for the world to know how we feel. We take and publish an endless stream of selfies, recreate every popular TikTok and pray to go viral, share our opinions in Instagram stories, and express ourselves in Snapchat photos. We blindly believe the world sees us as we see ourselves. In turn, this demanded self-expression in no way offers correction to others gone completely off the track of social decency, kindness, reason, and virtue.

Yes, my friends. It seems we live complacently in a world gone mad. The truth is, however, we can change how the world operates by having a love for others: a rejection of that which is unvirtuous, turning away from our self-importance, and a willingness to engage and discuss without spite those with whom we disagree. The pursuit of others for the purpose of their well-being in the relationship of friendship can be world-transforming when replicated by millions. Let's look at a noteworthy example. . . .

John Bunyan wrote *Pilgrim's Progress* while he was in prison for twelve years for the charge of not attending Anglican services and meeting with those outside of the Anglican Church. While in prison, he befriended other pastors imprisoned for the same reasons. These men supported one another and saw one another through the changing tides of public opinion, which finally led to their release. In his book, Bunyan's main character, Christian, is making his way to the Celestial City. He encounters many dangers and creatures attempting to impede his journey. Along the way, the most dangerous obstacles to his journey are other men and women. People with names like Talkative, Diffidence, Formalist, Hierocracy, Obstinate, and Pliable. These individuals attempt to lure him off his journey. The character of Christian, however, is helped by others with shared virtues, characters like Hopeful, Help, Charity, Prudence, Faithful, and others.[42]

The virtuous individuals in the story help Christian along his way, encourage him, guide him, and save him from peril. The unvirtuous are focused on themselves, their gains, and opportunities to find someone else to support them in their unvirtuous activity to provide affirmation. Bunyan knew what

---

42   John Bunyan, *The Pilgrim's Progress* (n.p.: Renaissance Classics, 2012).

the ancients knew: only the virtuous may have and know true friendship.

Friendship provides the solution for the modern man. We must step away from the overvalued constant connection to individuals online for brief encounters and replace it with our physical presence with those in our community or consistent connection through conversation with those near and far away. Real interactions, real concern, and real action can be formed by what we learn and know about them.

We must take an interest in our coworkers, neighbors, waiters, children, and spouses. We must learn the needs of those around us and fulfill them. We must extend an olive branch to learn and understand the questions and needs of our day and time. We must live and think virtuously and open our hearts and minds to others of virtue.

Connection between the generations can impart the wisdom needed to the younger generations to avoid the failures of the past while giving purpose and value to an aging generation. Our affection for one another will eliminate hate, not just of individuals but also of groups of individuals. Our communication across generational lines helps us understand the questions each generation is asking and provides an opportunity to offer, as Francis Schaefer called it, "honest answers to honest questions."[43]

---

43   Francis Schaeffer, *Two Contents, Two Realities* (Downers Grove, IL: InterVarsity Press, 1974), 15.

I feel the best honest answer is being virtuous. Hence, virtuous friendships lead to virtuous communities and the opportunity to invite others into productive social circles and relationships. The growth of virtuous communities becomes the spread of virtuous ideas and a return to the values long sought and lived out by the ancients. Consider the following from Boethius's *Consolation of Philosophy*:

> Avoid vice, Theodore, and cultivate virtues; lift up your mind to the right kind of hope, and put forth humble prayers on high. A great necessity is laid upon you, if you will be honest with yourself, a great necessity to be good, since you live in the sight of a judge who sees all things.[44]

I guess you could say that no good deed goes unpunished. This isn't to say the ancient world was perfect. Our world will not be perfect either, but the goal of goodness is a worthy pursuit in all ages. The virtues most sought by the ancients were courage, moderation, justice, and piety. These remain worthy pursuits in our day.

The Christian virtues are worthy of living out whether a believer in Christ or not—those virtues being prudence, justice, temperance, and fortitude with the three theological virtues of faith, hope, and charity. And there are the simple statements from Jesus about loving God and loving your neighbor in Mathew 22:37–39.

---

44   Boethius, *Consolation of Philosophy*, trans. V. E. Watts (London: Penguin Classics, 1969), bk. V, prose VI, 169.

Loving your neighbor must start now. The thing is, most people in your life will not commit to the intentional pursuit of others, so you must be the one to reach out. Your impact can be immense and touch thousands of lives with the care of just a few. Find a starting point and begin. Invite someone to lunch. Write a letter to a close friend and mail it. Call and ask with listening ears, "How are you?" Plan an adventure. Spend money on others. Offer counsel and seek counsel. Date your wife. And read the ancients, for they have answers we need to improve our world today.

RECOMMENDED READING

If you now have a desire to read the ancients and reflect on their thoughts and applications to the modern world and a desire to build friendships, I consider this book a success! Here are the ancient books I recommend you begin with:

Consolation of Philosophy — Boethius

Treatises on Friendship and Old Age — Cicero

On the Shortness of Life — Seneca

The Odyssey — Homer

The Republic — Plato

Mediations — Marcus Aurelius

Apology — Plato

The Nicomachean Ethics — Aristotle

Confessions — Augustine of Hippo

The Complete Poems — Catullus

The Book of Job — Unknown

Phaedo — Plato

The Rise and Fall of Athens—Nine Greek Lives — Plutarch

Crito — Plato

Elegies — Propertius

Psalms — Moses, Solomon, David, and others

Genesis — Moses

MESSAGE TO THE READER

I would be grateful for your feedback, and I am available to speak to you or your group about friendship. You may contact me by email or by visiting my website.

don@portroyalsocitety.org

www.donowens.com

Twitter: @donowens

Instagram: @donowens

Facebook: @donowens3

ABOUT THE AUTHOR

 **Don Owens** is president of The Port Royal Society, a U.S.-based non-profit organization promoting the reading and application of ancient books. He travels, speaking about his passion for books, people, and business at conferences for different companies, churches, and seminaries. He is also a CEO of an insurance group with offices in Fort Worth, Texas; Campeche and Merida, Mexico; San Pedro Sula, Honduras; and Managua, Nicaragua; he has served within this group for twenty-five years.

An avid outdoorsman, Don enjoys hiking, kayaking, and mountain and gravel biking. He spends a quarter of the year in Leadville, Colorado. He and David Rutherford cofounded The May Club, a men's fraternity focused on building friendships and sustaining relationships throughout life. The club is in its thirtieth year.

Don has been married to Danae Owens for thirty years. They have two children and one grandchild.